Rescue
from Beyond
the Roaring
Forties

Other titles of interest

The Loneliest Race
27,000 Miles Solo Around the World: the Story of the
BOC Challenge 1994–95
Paul Gelder
ISBN 0-7136-4202-5

The story of the men and one woman who took part in the ultimate endurance test, in which a motley group of amateurs on shoestring budgets pitted themselves against the top highly funded professionals of the sailing world. Only 20 of the 26 entrants crossed the start line, and by the halfway mark only 14 were left. This is an extraordinary story of courage, endurance and sheer determination by a remarkable group of individuals who were only too aware that in this race, simply to finish is to be a winner.

The Strange Last Voyage of Donald Crowhurst
Nicholas Tomalin and Ron Hall
ISBN 0-7136-4302-1

In 1968 Donald Crowhurst set out from Teignmouth, Devon in his untested trimaran, a competitor in the first singlehanded non-stop around the world race. Eight months later, the boat was found abandoned in a calm mid-Atlantic. Through Crowhurst's logs and diaries the world learned that, although he had radioed messages from his supposed round the world course, he had in fact never left the Atlantic. This journalistic masterpiece reconstructs Crowhurst's intriguing hoax to give us a suspenseful narrative and a psychological casebook of real zeal and anguish.

Sailing Alone Around the World
Capt Joshua Slocum
ISBN 0-7136-4539-3

Joshua Slocum's epic solo voyage around the world in 1895 in the 37ft sloop *Spray* stands as one of the greatest sea adventures of all time. It remains one of the major feats of singlehanded voyaging and has since been the inspiration for many who have gone to sea in small boats.

Starting from Boston on 24 April 1895, Slocum finally dropped anchor at Newport, Rhode Island on 27 June 1898. He had cruised some 46,000 miles entirely by sail and entirely alone – much of the time with the wheel lashed while he sat below reading or cooking or mending his clothes. Lovers of Slocum's adventure will welcome this new paperback edition.

RAPHAEL DINELLI

Rescue from Beyond the Roaring Forties

The story of Pete Goss's rescue of Raphael Dinelli

ADLARD COLES NAUTICAL
London

Published 1998 by Adlard Coles Nautical
an imprint of A & C Black (Publishers) Ltd
35 Bedford Row, London WC1R 4JH

Copyright © Anne Carrière Editions 1997

First published 1997 in French as
Raphael Dinelli: Pirate du Tour de Monde
by Anne Carrière Editions, Paris

ISBN 0 7136 4882 1

A CIP catalogue record for this book is available from
the British Library.

Translated from the French by Bill McDonald.

Typeset in 11.5 on 14pt Garamond Light
Printed and bound in Great Britain by
Cromwell Press, Melksham, Wiltshire

For Virginie and Philippine.
For that indefatigable and cheerful Mr Fixit, my father.
For my elder brother, family and friends.
For Guy, who works wonders for seafarers'
comfort and safety.

And, of course, For Pete.

Contents

• FOREWORD BY PETE GOSS •

When a fleet sets off round the world there is no pre-dicting what lies ahead, particularly in the reaches of the Southern Ocean. It is a lonely and desolate place, cold and grey, with little wildlife, shipping or indeed vapour trails.

I had many expectations at the start of the Vendée Globe Challenge, and had visualised every scenario both good and bad. However the last thing I expected was to make a close and lifelong friend in the most testing experience of my life. The rescue of Raphael Dinelli from the face of certain death was a team effort that started on Christmas Day.

Many things contributed to Raphael's survival, the most important, and perhaps unrecognised, was Raphael's incred-ible determination to live. Quite how he pushed life before him for so long escapes imagination.

Pulling him on board was the best Christmas present of my life, and it was a present. I had no idea what I was unwrap-ping as his survival suit was slowly and painfully eased off. He could have been anything; life is not a fairy tale.

Raphael was on board for ten days as we made our way to his drop off in Hobart. During that time we bridged the language barrier and cemented a firm friendship that will transcend time and geography; he is like a brother.

Since my return I have had the privilege of being his best man and we are to compete together in a two handed trans-Atlantic yacht race.

He is a good man; it was a privilege to save his life. And I am sure it will continue to be fulfilling, if only because of his experience to date which he has shared with us in this book.

Fair winds Raphael – you deserve them.

Les Sables d'Olonne, 17 February, 1997

In the midst of an incredible fleet of craft of every kind, filling the port's approach channel, one alone is under sail: Christophe Auguin's *Geodis*, victor in an inimitable 105 days' passage of the Vendée Globe challenge – around the world, singlehanded, without a port of call, without assistance. It is a triumphal return, mainsail still set, proud as any battle ensign, under the eyes of a jubilant crowd of tens of thousands. And I am glad for Christophe, as a champion and as a friend. But for me, it is a bitter-sweet moment. A little over three months earlier I was at the helm of *Algimouss*, outward bound down this same channel, facing the same challenge. How could I have imagined then that some Southern Ocean Santa Claus, greybeard lord of the 50th parallel, would mark the 25th December by putting an end to my voyage, and send my vessel two days later 3500 metres down to the ocean floor?

And so it was that I was not to enjoy my moment of triumph, returning as a circumnavigator one winter's day to Les Sables; the end of a dream. Not that it would have been a victor's return; that much I knew. And yet I should have been able to say to myself, 'You've done it; you've seen it through to the end.' The Vendée Globe has another name among lone voyagers; we call it the Everest of the oceans.

Not that even this does justice to the challenge, to the magnitude of the undertaking.

I was asked once, 'When do you know that you've made it, that you've won?' I replied that as far as I was concerned, it began and ended in the same place, between the harbour entrance buoys. Not on the finishing line. In that sense, perhaps it is like the conquest of Everest. And why? Because all along the banks of the entrance channel, when you set out and when you return, carrying you along on the sheer spirit of their support, there is this crowd of thousands, and they are one with you, and you with them.

On that November day at the start, though, I was the last of the fleet to leave, and I remember how the cheering crowd made me forget for a moment the slap in the face I had been given the day before by the race organisers, who had refused to recognise my entry. The crowds still cheered me, perhaps now as an outsider, as a privateer, and I should have liked to have thanked them by my return at *Algimouss'* helm. But it was not to be. Not that this will be the end of the story; I promise them that I will do it again. It is the ultimate adventure, and has become my reason for living. Whatever happens to our world, I am convinced that these long distance races will continue, and that the participating craft will become yet faster, and thus safer, whatever the critics may say. Any skipper will tell you the same; the faster the boat, the better your chance of escaping a storm. That will be my objective, too; the initial ideas are clear in my mind, and I have begun to commit them to paper.

The next time, though, I will set out to win, and no two ways about it. Victory is a powerful driving force capable of seeing us through the worst extremes. Last time, I was able to set out to complete the course, but not to win. If, next time, I do not set out to win, it will not be worth setting out at all. I don't want to hear the reassuring, 'You're still young, you've time to gain experience.' What if I am? I've worked for this for years. After what I've already been through in the

Southern Ocean, what more experience could one ask for? A Hollywood epic with special effects?

The evening Auguin came ashore at Les Sables, we talked it all over; one seaman to another. 'I've seen the pictures of when you went down,' he told me. 'It was horrendous. Whether the skipper was you or anyone else. It made a deep impression on me.' His words gave me a fresh input of energy, coming from an old hand, victor of three major singlehanded races. One day I shall be an old hand. Even now, I think my experiences have made me something different from the mad teenager who scared his mother silly when he made his first passages across the Bay of Arcachon on a sailboard.

CHAPTER 1

Force 10 in the bay

So often, a grown-up will ask a child, 'What do you want to be one day?' I don't really remember what my own reply was. I don't think that at that stage I really knew. Artist or hell's angel, airline pilot or seafarer? I didn't know. Come to that, I don't really remember my earlier years very well; I always felt that my life began, properly speaking, when I was a little older. For the record, I was born at Floirac, south-west France, in May 1968, a time when earth-shaking events seemed to be going on in France. My own earth-shaking events would come rather later!

My father had been a marine engineer, but by the time I was growing up, he worked at Aerospatiale, building rocket motors. It was work that he found fascinating; my mother, like many Frenchwomen in those years, made a career of bringing up my sister, my brother and myself. I don't remember my early years at Floirac very well; my most abiding memory and my most formative influence was provided some kilometres away, by the bay of Arcachon, where my mother's parents lived and where we spent our summer holidays. It was there that I learned the way of the tides and the sea, swimming in the creeks, finding my way around the little angling boat in which my father and uncle spent their summer days. It wasn't a very adventurous apprenticeship, far less, say, than most young Bretons experience; they become natural seamen very early on. At that stage I think I was more of an apprentice to my father, who loved cars, Alfa Romeos in particular, and would rebuild them, cannibalising crashed vehicles. With him I progressed from being a 'stand and hold it' to a young mechanic. His work brought him into contact with the latest materials, some of which found their way home, so that I was able to experiment with polyurethane foam, carbon fibre and so on long before most boatyards did; in fact that was the material I used for the first boat I built, a little tub to row about the creeks.

It was a little after this – I would have been ten years old – when my great formative experience arrived. My father and uncle had been asked to evaluate something completely new in the sailing world, the first sailboards. They were bigger and heavier than today's, and trying them for myself, it took all my strength to raise the pivoting rig and get under way. That summer we took the boards down to Arcachon, and my father and uncle, orthodox sailors, couldn't get on with them at all. I found myself doing most of the evaluating, and fell in love with boardsailing. It was an affair that was to last for more than ten years.

In that same year, 1978, I had another formative experience, when I watched the end of the first Route Du Rhum race, and Mike Birch pipped Michel Malinovski at the post off Pointe-à-Pitre. It was fantastic: they had taken radically different routes, and yet here they were, arriving at the same landfall within minutes of each other! I was fascinated by Malinovski's great rocket of a monohull, and the trimaran in which Birch had beaten him. It signalled a revolution in ocean racing, and I recognised it. If there was one moment at which I was bitten by the bug, it was then.

Between my tenth and eighteenth year, every summer was given over to boardsailing at Andernos, and it was there that I made my first open sea passages across to Arcachon town and back before the tide ebbed and left me and a few friends to drag our boards back across the mudflats, which was how we ended up more than once. Those were happy days, and they were early days for windsurfing. We were in at the beginning, and we were at the leading edge.

I began to deal in boards in a small way, and importantly, to design and build them. It was a good learning experience, and in this way that I discovered the nearby Pyla sailing club not far from Europe's highest sand dune. Finding myself among other enthusiasts I was taken on as an assistant instructor; I was just fourteen. From that summer on, I would start the season by sailing across from Andernos to Pyla, on my big old board, with my kit and camping gear in water-tight bags. I liked that. The other instructors would arrive from Brittany or Paris in their station wagons, with their boards on the roof. I arrived on my board.

A tent on a beach was far from being an ideal workshop, but each summer I would try to develop my boards a little more. I built shorter, lighter prototypes, and I introduced carbon fibre. Not that the summer provided ideal test conditions; a light land or sea breeze wasn't enough to experiment with ultimate performance. I waited impatiently for the depressions that worked their way down from Brittany and the Channel. And when they came, girlfriends and parties could wait on shore; I would be out in the wild surf, testing the board and myself to the limit.

There were boardsailing competitions at that time, but I didn't find them a serious challenge because they were really for summer sailors in light winds. In fact they were frustrating. A few of us, just a very few, preferred to go out in hard conditions, conditions when no-one else was out – even with a force 9 or 10 forecast and spindrift everywhere. If it wasn't plainly suicidal, we would go out and chance our arm.

Until I was eighteen years old my board was my only form of transport. As I grew up, I have to admit I found it a little limiting. I would have liked a motor bike, but my parents flatly refused. My father dangled an alternative carrot: 'If you work hard at your studies, you can have a car for your eighteenth birthday.' A car was more than a symbol of adulthood and freedom; it would be a passport to more demanding sailing waters than the Arcachon. At that time I was deep into the boardsailing magazines that took me in my imagination to magic coasts. I didn't think of a car as transport to discos, but as a means of getting my boards and gear to where the wind blew and the surf roared. When the holiday sailors stayed ashore, that's when I would set out. And so it was that I worked hard enough to pass my accountancy exams – and my car duly arrived, a Renault 4 estate. From then on it would inevitably resemble a mobile chandler's store.

I would have liked to be able to Live to Sail and Sail to Live; but life isn't like that. There is also the matter of study and eventually work. I had enrolled at a technical institute for a diploma level course, but I had chosen an establishment within easy reach of the Atlantic coast. When an interesting weather system was in the offing, I would turn up for lectures in foul weather gear, board on the roof of my car, ready to go as soon as work was over.

There were a few other sailboard fanatics on the same course; sometimes we would be away for two or three days and get back without having slept. The lecturers seemed to understand. One of them once remarked, on our return, 'We were worried about you, it was blowing hard.' There was a sort of gentlemen's agreement between staff and ourselves. We looked nothing like accountancy students, and would miss lectures on and off, but we were expected to turn in exam and assessment results of at least 50 per cent. If not, there would be trouble. And so that is what we did. Sometimes I had to revise shut away like a mad monk to get my 50 per cent result, but I always achieved it.

At the end of my first year's studies, I returned to Pyla for another summer as an instructor, but I was dreaming; dreaming of distant coasts, distant girls, but above all of distant seas. September came, and I was free. The summer courses at the sailing club were over, and our new term was not due to begin until October. I loaded the car and set out for southern Spain; it was my first long voyage.

• CHAPTER 2 •

Dinelli? Who the hell does he think he is?

The Straits of Gibraltar. Sun and wind; lots of wind at that, sometimes force 9 and 10. And life was one long fiesta. I was just eighteen and this was ultimate boardsailing country. Ultimate sailing, pure sailing, faster, further, more dangerous. And after a few days of this, I found I was fixing my eyes increasingly on the Moroccan coast. The Other Side? At that time, no-one had ever attempted a sailboard crossing. And each evening my friend François and I would say to each other, 'Tomorrow, we'll try it!' It wasn't just to be the first to do it; it was something beyond that. It was the same call that I had felt as a little lad, when I prepared for my first crossing of the bay of Arcachon. I think it's an essential part of me, and that it will remain with me.

But the Straits of Gibraltar are in a different league from the bay of Arcachon. There are ships, there are sharks, there is the current and the wind, and above all a six or seven metre swell. And in the end, I didn't try. Perhaps the sense of self-preservation was stronger than the call of the Straits and the distant shore.

A year later I passed my final exam, just well enough to be able to feel that I had succeeded in combining my sailing with my studies. I put in one more summer as an instructor and then, in September, I set off again, this time for the

Canaries. I was alone, with the little Renault loaded down with my board and gear. The police and customs didn't like the look of it one bit, and made me unload the lot; they were convinced that I might be carrying drugs, if not in the boards themselves, then perhaps in the tins of resin and acetone which always travelled with me.

I've laughed ever since at the holiday industry's presentation of the Canaries. They all show dream beaches, dream hotels and the rest of the dream. But the Canaries aren't like that at all; they are wild and volcanic, perhaps with the exception of Santa Cruz. There is so much wind that the hotel swimming pools are situated below sea level to give them a little shelter. All the tourists are concentrated in what amounts to a concrete fortress, and the board sailors, people that I would have expected to be more adventurous, crowded to the extent of perhaps two hundred sails in one bay. Yes, there were magnificent launching spots, but they were dangerous. The lava sea bed shelves, and the surf breaks. Very dangerous in places, but allowing fantastic surfing. I learned this not the hard way but at second hand when I went to the rescue of a local board sailor; he was taken to hospital with a foot half torn off by the rocks. The locals had even talked of blowing up some of the more dangerous reefs and pinnacles. I had one advantage over most touring sailors, though; I had brought my 'mobile workshop', and could repair what damage I did to my board.

It was here that my life could have taken a turn in an entirely different direction. At that time a sort of sailboard and funboard World Cup was taking place, and one of the press took some film footage of me and showed it to some of the German community who have been part of Canaries life for the last twenty-five years with their Surf Shops. They invited me to stay on with them as a professional. With their sponsorship, I could have competed at international level. But I was more interested in freedom; all I wanted at that time was to sail till I was exhausted and then collapse. I was so exhausted at times that I would sleep long, long hours in the car, recovering. Then there was the fact that I was living on a cheap basic diet of tomatoes, rice and so on, and to sail to professional competition standard I would have had to eat more expensively than that. Ultimately I suppose I wasn't yet mature enough to cope with the discipline of a training regime. Yes, I could have travelled as a professional, to Hawaii and the other places, but at that stage I was content to sail for my own enjoyment, demanding enjoyment though it might be.

That was a time of adventure and of great development in boardsailing, and I was there. Perhaps we were a little mad; we would see a five or six metre breaking sea, and wonder what would happen if a board jumped from the crest – and then we'd try it. That was where the Killer Loop was invented, before even the Hawaiians tried anything of the kind. But it was also a time of loss of simplicity. I was one of the top board sailors of my time, but my only income was what I had made as an instructor, and world class boardsailing was already growing very expensive. To stay on top, we had to take risks to the extent that we were damaging a great deal of gear. This was what brought me to a crossroads in my life; the equipment was developing so fast that I couldn't keep up on my own funds. It was the first time I had really encountered the importance of money in sport, and it was a bugbear which would snap at my heels from that time onward.

What now, then? I had turned down what the Canaries had to offer. Which way should I go? It has to be said that in the early 1980s in France, a boardsailing background amounted to a handicap to anyone wanting to enter the offshore racing world. The French yachting establishment was traditionalist and snobbish; for the big class yachties, board sailors were yobbos who upset swimmers and would surely kill someone one day. And of course I was one of those yobbos. The yacht club fraternity regarded me in the same way that tennis snobs would regard an inner city kid who showed enough talent to take them on but had never had any expensive coaching. I think they have regarded me, some of them, in this way ever since. I upset them, that's certain, but I hope I also made them sit up and take notice.

I don't have to live down my boardsailing background. In fact, I owe a great deal to it. Without the experience it gave me, I doubt I should have been able to stand up to the physical experience of being wrecked in those conditions in the Southern Ocean. When my boat was going down in a force 10, I was able to say to myself, 'Come on, it's not the first time you've been freezing and surrounded by breaking seas, and it's not your first mouthful of cold salt water.' I know it isn't exactly in the same league, but I think to a great extent it was my boardsailing years that came to the rescue.

But although I was still sailing whenever I could, I had to work. I started as a salesman for a company making carpet cleaning products and machines, which I had to repair on site when they broke down, which was often. It was hard, and stressful, and I ended up having a shouting match with the general manager. A second job proved a happier experience, selling again, but toys this time. It was still hard and the hours were long. I would be away for days at a stretch, and wasn't getting the exercise I needed; in the end I bought a rowing machine which I would take up to my hotel room each night.

At weekends I was making a start in offshore racing as a crewman on a Class 8 boat out of Arcachon. It was demanding, and the level of the competition was high; I learned a great deal. Then, at the Pyla club, I met a girl called Virginie... But I was trying to cram too much into my life. Driving long hours, I gave myself one or two bad frights, especially after the lunchtime drinking sessions which were obligatory for French sales reps until recently. In the end, I had to make a break. I resigned from the job and took a retraining grant which was available for a professionals' course at the National Sailing School at Quiberon. I lived in a van, converted very basically, and drove back to Arcachon at weekends to be with Virginie. At the end of my two year course I came out with the best result of my year, and returned to Arcachon as a full-time instructor. It felt good, but at the same time I knew that it was not something I could do for the rest of my life.

A new door opened to me, however, when Thierry Eluere, builder of the first boat to win the Vendée Globe in 1990, offered me a job in his yard, and I found myself refitting the same boat for the 1992 race under a new owner-skipper. I was told what needed doing, and given a free hand to go ahead and do it. Once again, I learned a great deal in the course of this work, but more importantly it was my first taste of a world class ocean racer. I think it was there that I made up my mind that one day I would sail the Vendée Globe. One day... I was close to tears when that boat finally left the yard; it had become part of my life.

Until then, although I had crewed in offshore races, I wasn't really known in the yachting fraternity. And as I said before, I still had the reputation of a beach bum with a sailboard. It was true that I still had a great deal to learn, but I was learning all the same, and now I had a specific goal; to be an offshore racing skipper myself. Virginie and I worked on at the yard for a year after 'my' boat's departure. We lived in my van to save on rent. And all the while, I was turning over in my mind the things I had learned from that boat, and from her builder and skipper.

There is a French race which amounts to a qualifying stage for international ocean racing; the 'Figaro' singlehanded challenge. It takes place each August and is a series of passage races in 9.15 metre boats. It is a great challenge physically, a struggle not only against the sea but against lack of sleep. There is a different course each year, but basically it is within the cruising ground of Brittany, Ireland and

Spain. Thus it takes in the Channel, the Irish Sea and the Atlantic, to say nothing of Biscay; not waters to fool around in, and the most demanding of them all, in summer, is the Irish Sea. I decided I was going to attempt it. That was where the great names all started, and it was where I would start too.

This meant finding a boat. It was at this point that my old friend François Hardy, who had been with me in Spain, came to my aid, not least with some good advice. He was now in an executive post in a big company, and he had seen something of the reaction of his own bosses to young offshore skippers seeking sponsorship. He told me what they always said; it amounted to 'Look, young man, it all sounds very promising, but you haven't a boat of your own. We don't doubt that you would be in with a chance of winning, but you must understand that from our point of view the Figaro isn't the Vendée Globe, and it really wouldn't bring us the advantage we would expect if we sponsored you, so all we can do is wish you good luck.' In other words, we had first of all to find a boat.

So it was that one winter's day, in January 1993, we went down to the port of St-Gilles Croix-de-Vie, to look over a 9.15 metre boat which had already taken part in two Figaro races. She was for sale for 300,000 francs. I didn't have that kind of money. So, with François' help I went after smaller sources of sponsorship and help, a little here, a little there. In the end it was all done on borrowed money, any actual funds of our own going on sails, insurance and the rest. At the time I was only working part-time for the port of Arcachon, and earning what extra I could on repairing boats and so on. I was fired with enthusiasm to start, and that involved getting to know the boat a little better. This would have been best accomplished by taking part in the different French singlehanded championships which effectively lead up to the Figaro, but I simply didn't have the money to do it that way.

In the end, the first race I entered was the Brest event. I had the boat well in hand, and the cruise from Arcachon up to Brest gave me more valuable experience. I think I've had an advantage in that I've always had to sail from my home port to the starting point of a race; I must have put in some thousands of miles of singlehanded passage-making in this way, and it was excellent training. When I arrived in Brest in May 1993 all the great names of French offshore single-handed racing were already there. When we started, there was a 40 knot wind, and it was wild; boats were losing their masts a few metres away from me, and this was before we were even clear of the Rade de Brest. I tell you, it was a hairy way to make a start! But the conditions were just what I wanted; it was the kind of wind I'd liked best when board-sailing. I was planing, I was flying, and I forgot the champions racing a cable or so away. I sailed my own race, and I think I sailed it well, as I finished seventh out of a field of fifteen or sixteen. And inevitably, after the race, I heard the malicious mutterings of 'Just who the hell does Dinelli think he is?'

You'll find out, you bastards, I thought. You'll find out.

• CHAPTER 3 •

Next year, around the world

Ever since my Quiberon days, my answer to the question 'Where are you from then?' seemed to mark me down in the eyes of the Bretons, who imagine themselves as France's only real sailors, as a farm boy with hayseeds in my ears. Later one skipper, who might have known better, Olivier de Kersauson, nearly came to blows with me.

'Arcachon? ARCACHON? The queers' capital of the Atlantic coast! No tides, and no bloody seamen! You're a bunch of brothel-creepers south of the Loire! And what have you done offshore? The poxy Figaro? Any dolly bird could walk it!' And with that he invited me to come and have a drink!

Perhaps they thought I was still wet behind the ears, but all during 1993 I was climbing their ladder. Brest had given me the green light. I had found I wasn't afraid, I didn't ask myself deep questions, except perhaps on the financial front – I just got stuck in. I had found a little sponsorship, which was encouraging, but we were still sleeping in the van while the other competitors slept in hotels ashore, and overnight in port Virginie and I would like as not be working on some problem or other with the boat. But the next morning I would still be off, and still in high spirits.

The end of July came, and I crossed the start line of the Figaro at St-Malo. La Coruña, Douarnenez, Kinsale, Fastnet, finishing at St Quay-Portrieux, North Brittany – it would be a good initiation, especially the notorious Fastnet. In the event, when we put into Kinsale, I was steering manually; every electrical system on board had gone down. I crossed the finishing line fourteenth out of thirty; not bad for a first try. On top of that, I was second among the contestants sailing the Figaro for a first time, and it is a fact that the first three first-time Figaro contestants are usually men with a future in offshore racing. On the debit side, I had learned what fatigue can do to a singlehanded skipper. I had thought at one point that the stars were the navigation lights of a ship bearing down on me. It was my first hallucinatory experience at sea.

So 1993 was a good year. I had turned in some good racing results, learned more about myself, found my confidence. When I docked at the end of the Figaro I don't know who looked more radiantly happy, Virginie or myself.

Now I was really part of the racing circuit. But it was not without stirring up a little jealousy and animosity. One or two Arcachon skippers still seeking sponsorship weren't at all happy that I'd succeeded in buying a boat, even less so when the regional administration invited me to race under their colours. Then there were the old stuffed shirts of the yacht clubs, who didn't like the presence in their world of a beach bum who lived in a van. Some of them actually booed me when I sailed from Arcachon. It reduced Virginie to tears. I suppose there will always be people like that; a pity.

Financially, on the other hand, 1993 had been nothing special. I had brought in a total of 150,000 francs, and it wasn't enough to make ends meet. I suppose for a first year it wasn't bad, but it wasn't enough. Everything seemed to be swallowed up by the boat, and we lived from hand to mouth. It was to become a familiar experience. The following year was better, bringing as it did a certain amount of practical recognition of my racing results, which were still good. I was made manager of the Arcachon sailing base, on

a part-time basis which would enable me to continue training and racing. This was more like it, and I was able to
return the town's favour in small measure by organising the
first Arcachon offshore event that same year.

Less successful was my first two-handed transatlantic race
– not from a racing point of view but because my opposite
number, who should have met half the expenses, defaulted.
It put me out of sorts enough to affect my Figaro effort the
following month; out of a field of forty I could not manage
better than twenty-fifth. Worse was to come; my contract at
the sailing base was not renewed, Virginie was pregnant, we
were living in what amounted to a bedsit, and there was still
the boat to keep up. I had just finished paying for it, but its
upkeep didn't cost any less. On top of it all, the winter was
the coldest for years.

The following year was a gamble at long odds. I was on
the dole, only one of my sponsors had stayed with me, and
I would have to make one supreme effort as a full-time
racing skipper or go down altogether. The pressure was
enormous, as this years' Figaro was to start from Arcachon,
from home, and the only new sponsors I could find had put
very demanding conditions on their support. I was to finish
placed tenth or better, and had to be first over the line of the
six other local competitors. There were fifty-two boats taking
part, and a line-up of top skippers. It was a case of winner
take all, and no replay.

All that winter I worked like a madman on the boat. Single-
handedly I lowered the keel and added to it 40 kilos of lead,
using a theodolite to realign it. Everything had to be accurate
to the last millimetre on account of the strict rating rules, and
I don't know of many Figaro contestants who have done this
themselves! Nor were the working conditions very easy. In
winter there could be 10 centimetres of water swirling round
my feet. I hired a young drifter to give me a hand, and to
enable the resin to cure I needed to heat the polytent we were
working in – 380 volts of power on, and rainwater every-

where... After three weeks, the police came down and took the boy away, and I was left singlehanded again.

Finally it was summer, and the die was almost cast. A week before the race we lifted the boat for sanding and polishing; a racing hull must be perfectly smooth. It was very hot, and I got some anti-fouling dust in my ear. The result was a painful infection and a stiff course of antibiotics. I knew they would pull me down physically, and they did. I could forget about being in top condition for the race, but there was nothing to be done; we would just have to see.

The day we were due to start I had lunch with Philippe Poupon. At forty, he was the king of the offshore skippers, and had nothing more to prove to himself. He also ranked high in my estimation because he likes to encourage young skippers; but what he had to say to me was astounding. 'Raphael, I'll make you an offer. If you come in among the first ten, I'll sell you my boat so you can sail in next year's Vendée Globe.' This was not just any old boat; when Philippe had sailed her in the last Vendée Globe, he had finished second.

There was only one possible reply: 'You're on!' Philippe had judged me capable of taking part in the queen of races, the Vendée Globe.

The moment of truth had arrived. I crossed the start line still unwell from the antibiotics. I don't consider I made a particularly good start, which must have pleased the yachties in their blazers. But Philippe's proposition had given me a powerful impetus. Just as well; none of us knew that this first leg, to Kinsale via the Fastnet, would be a passage to remember. I was one of the first into the thick of it, a depression of a depth that takes some imagining. The following year, after rounding the Horn in the Vendée Globe, skipper Gerry Roufs was to say to a radio audience, 'It wasn't that bad. The first leg of Figaro 95 was much worse.'

The Western approaches were transformed into something I can only describe as apocalyptic, with moments of calm more menacing than the worst gust. The thunder and lightning were like something out of another world, and with 35 and 40 knots of wind the boat was hurled about like a toy ball. Then all would fall calm. After a moment's pause it would all start again. I have never seen anything remotely like it.

Most of the fifty-two boats taking part were within view, and the sights I saw were like something out of Hieronymus Bosch. A ghastly illumination of lightning flashes played over the fleet. There was thunder everywhere and lightning strikes to masts on every hand. I suffered a near miss, and I tell you I was afraid – not just for myself, but for the boat's electronics. It was hot, and I was wearing just a T-shirt. Suddenly there was water flying everywhere. I was below at this point, and afraid to go on deck. For fear of what might happen, I shut down the main circuit and isolated the batteries. This, of course, put the autopilots out of action. Then came a gust that laid us on our beam ends, and I realised that it was down to me to get on the helm and bring her under control. I made for the cockpit on all fours, in T-shirt and long johns, and took the helm as the lightning struck all around me like a spitting dragon. It was beyond description. Talking to highly experienced skippers afterwards, none could recall an experience like it; and the relief when it was over beggars description.

After that, I didn't do too badly. For the next three days, I sailed on within sight of Poupon, and we raced tack for tack. At one point, though, when we were some three miles apart, he called me up on the radio.

'Raphael, come about! There's a submarine on a collision course with you. I'm leaving him away to port!' I thought he was pulling my leg; it's not unknown between friends when racing. A submarine? If he wasn't joking, was it the fatigue making him see things? I came about, to close on him and see if he was OK, when I saw it. He was right. It was a submarine trimmed down with just the conning tower showing, and making about 25 to 30 knots! He seemed to be making right for me. Surely there was someone on watch! In less time than it takes to describe what happened, he went slicing past, missing me by no more than a few metres. I tell you, it brought me out in a sweat: I had had some near misses with whales, and that's an experience you remember. But a submarine – I could just imagine the headlines: 'Figaro skipper abandons ship after being hit by a submarine!'

The English Channel and the Irish Sea are in some ways a more difficult proposition than the Southern Ocean, where the main hazard is ice. Apart from whales and submarines, there are the ships. Radar isn't permitted under the Figaro rules, and the race takes place along the same maritime motorway that these great juggernauts have to keep to by international law. They are no more likely to give way to a little yacht than an elephant is to a mouse, so it is up to us to judge their course and speed and keep out of their way. And remember, an unnecessary change of course or tack may lose you the race. On the other hand, we are acutely aware of the casualties there have been, in the Figaro alone, as a result of collisions with ships, to say nothing of other ocean races.

On that first leg, Arcachon–Kinsale, I finished seventh; Poupon was second. I wasn't too unhappy. I think if I hadn't had to shut down my navionics for a while to rest a shaky battery, I might have stayed up with him. Once again there was that nagging reminder of the role of money in competition. A battery isn't a great consideration if you have the money to replace it. I was glad for Poupon, anyway, as a decent skipper who doesn't employ dirty racing tactics, like so many. I'm with him; I race to win, but I won't treat it as a fight to the death with no holds barred.

Throughout the subsequent legs of the race I managed to hold my position, despite the continuing nagging drain of the infection and the medication. When I crossed the line at Brest it was a close finish, just as sometimes happens in the

Tour de France: Poupon was first on corrected time, though I just managed to beat him boat for boat, and he gave me a cheer and a wave as I crossed the line. On corrected time I was tenth: I had *just* fulfilled my sponsorship conditions. I don't think the yachting journalists quite understood why Poupon came up to me to congratulate the man who had come tenth. They didn't know that it meant he was going to sell me his boat, and that the next year it would be the big one – the Vendée Globe!

• CHAPTER 4 •

Breaking the bank

Until that moment, I think that participating in the Vendée Globe had remained no more than a dream for me, an ambition about which I had talked only to a few close friends. After Poupon's promise. I was free to transform that dream into reality. The return cruise to Arcachon was something of a triumph and, unusually, I shared it with a party of friends; it was more like a holiday cruise than the sort of sailing I was used to.

It was early September 1995. The race would begin in the November of the next year, so I had no more than a year to prepare; most of the contestants start three, even four years before. From now on, every day would have to be dedicated to preparations; there was no time to lose. That meant there was no question of taking part in other races meantime so, of course, no Figaro 1996. I would miss it, and the other races with their atmosphere and camaraderie.

For my own part I was still the Shoestring Skipper; I wasn't working, and sponsorship certainly didn't run to engaging a professional rigger, as do some. My father had joined in as 'Support Team', bringing my van with spares and tools to each port of call in a race; I owe him a great deal. I obtained help from enthusiastic teenagers, and could pay their expenses, but no more than that. My father, the former Merchant Service officer, would roust them out of their sleeping bags after a night on the town. During races I didn't have time for a night on the town, even during the Figaro, when big celebrations are laid on for the contestants. I made an exception, though, for the Jameson centre, Ireland's whiskey temple. There are such things as priorities, after all! Sometimes the boys would be too hung-over to turn out and work, and I found myself doing their job as well; thank goodness Virginie always came too – there was nothing to which she couldn't turn her hand. And once again, I found myself my father's helpmate. 'Raphael – got a 13 mm socket? And can you stick the charger on?' If I owe my sponsors much, I owe my loved ones more.

As a singlehanded skipper, I regretted that little of my sailing could be shared with Virginie. One adventure that she did share, however, turned out very differently from anything we had expected. Back in 1994, after the arrival of the two-way Transatlantic race, the Lorient-St-Barthélemy, I had to return the boat to Point-à-Pitre to be loaded aboard a ship. Virginie came to join me for that one, and she was unlucky because we encountered head winds of 30–35 knots. We were turning to windward and the boat was heavily loaded, as I had two full sets of racing stores and equipment aboard. Poor Virginie became seasick, very seasick. She stuck on an anti-seasickness patch, but we hadn't realised that she was allergic, and instead of making her a little woozy it sent her into a drugged sleep.

Inevitably at this point the ballast tank started leaking, and I had to bail out 200 litres of water from the cabin. Each time I went about I had to transfer Virginie to the lee berth, and move some hundreds of kilos of stores up to windward. It was a better training session than many gyms could provide!

Finally, night fell. I switched on the radio and navigation lights. Shortly afterwards I saw first one, then another craft under sail without lights, which I found odd; perhaps, I though, that was what the locals commonly did, not that it was particularly safe. Some time after that, I saw a trawler with a large deck cargo hidden under a tarpaulin. No light and radio silence again. I wondered what the cargo was; it certainly wasn't fish. A friend of mine had once told me that he never sailed unarmed, as down in the Grenadines he had narrowly avoided being boarded by pirates, or at least criminals, and the islands were swarming with such types. Worse still, the trawler now followed me, lights still out, for half an hour.

Over the radio I heard several suspicious messages in what might be called veiled speech. By this time I was really frightened, and switched off my navigation lights and radio. Virginie was still out cold. For the next 48 hours I made to windward, by the end hardly able to keep my eyes open, until we made landfall at Point-à-Pitre. There, I can only say I hit the rum with relief. I think the fumes may even have revived Virginie, who awoke fresh as a daisy, and when we went ashore danced the night away!

Perhaps that ought to be how I earned my nickname of 'the pirate'. At least it all turned out happily; and I think it marked the end of what I call my apprenticeship as a single-handed skipper. So in that sense I had the right to feel ready for the Vendée Globe. Why not?

Back in La Rochelle I went to see Philippe Poupon's boat, with which he had sailed the first Vendée Globe. She was a monohull, ketch rigged, a little on the heavy side but very sound. The asking price was 1½ million francs. I didn't have that number of centimes, so I had to get the money together somehow, as this was going to be my boat. I went down to see her several times, working through all her hidden corners, examining the details of hull and rig. All the time I was saying to myself, 'This is the one'. I think I fell in love with the 60 foot veteran.

But still I had to find the money, and I was far from being able to do so. I was out of work, with rent to pay, and of course there was now little Philippine, who had been born some months previously. With a well-received Figaro result just behind me, I sought new sponsors, and managed to interest the owner of a chain of hairdressing businesses across south-west France; he alone doubled the amount available. I now had a workable budget: three million francs. Half of that would buy the boat, and the campaign would account for the rest. I contacted Poupon who was down at St-Barthelémy, his usual home when he wasn't somewhere in the Southern Ocean. He replied by sending me a sale agreement. We had made a start.

The sale was to be completed a week before the Paris Boat Show in December. I had already contacted the race organiser, Philippe Jeantot, with a resumé of a racing record, but had yet to notify him officially of my entry for the Vendée Globe. I should have learned by then not to count my chicks before they were hatched; the hairdressing magnate contacted me just a few days before the sale.

'Look, I'm sorry, but I'm going to have to withdraw.' It was the old story of a divorce settlement, and his wife's lawyers had got their claws on the collateral. This was serious; all my plans went west. Ten months to go to the race, funds for the campaign conditional on my obtaining a boat, and my own boat chartered to another racing skipper. In other words, I was neck deep in the proverbial.

Poupon put his cards on the table. He had already missed a sale two years earlier in similar circumstances. He confirmed that I could still have the boat, but if anyone turned up with the money before me...

Someone did. It was Bertrand de Broc. I had reached a low ebb, and it wasn't a Merry Christmas. I began to cast about for another boat and another sponsor. Yes, there were boats for sale, but the pick of the fleet had already found a buyer. Those that remained were either known slow old tubs or rust buckets. All the same, I set out on a tour of the ports of France on what still looked like a wild goose chase. I had been offered insurance on whatever boat I found, so an alternative possibility was to charter a boat. It was an outside chance though, as most vendors would far rather sell than charter. Nothing seemed likely to turn up, but I had little choice so I kept on looking.

While passing through Les Sables d'Olonne, I had looked at Philippe Jeantot's *Crédit Agricole*, and we had already discussed the possibility of me buying her, although I had continued looking as she was not ideal for me. So I returned to Jeantot, and we discussed possibilities again – and this time reached an agreement. He knew how keen I was to take part in the race, and that I had funds on hand for the campaign. So at last we could make a start. There was not a minute to lose, for now I had not only to refit the boat but to modify her, and this as cheaply as possible – which is seldom the best way – but it was all I could do.

Jeantot's boat was very well designed and her hull and spars were sound, but she was far from being a modern boat, and she was heavy. We decided to strip her to her essentials; for example three quarters of her winches and other deck gear were taken out. We changed the keel, the shrouds, the boom, the obsolete electronics, and at the end of it all the middle aged lady had become a dolly bird. Her original thirteen tonnes displacement were down to ten, and this despite the addition of two tonnes to her keel! I would have liked to have gone further with the stripping down, but fortunately there was neither the time nor the money – fortunately, because her multiple watertight bulkheads and heavy internal hatches, which made her look like a battleship alongside modern boats, were to be a key contributing factor to my survival less than a year later.

Between March, when Jeantot and I reached agreement, and 3 November, the starting date, the suspense was terrible as I was unable to find another major sponsor until very near the end. The former skipper of *Crédit Agricole* had promised to find one, but that came to nothing. By mid-October my boat was still in pieces, the hull at Arcachon, the mast down south at Lunel, the keel in the Vendée, and the sails and most of the electronics at La Rochelle! Worse, none of the subcontractors for the work would deliver until they were paid, and I could not do this until a matter of weeks before the start – in fact a bare two weeks before the qualifying race. At the last moment the managing director of Algimouss, a company whose nearest connection with the sea is its maintenance products for swimming pools, came up with a desperately needed million frances. The weeks that followed felt like the maddest campaign in the history of sail.

It had already taken a month's hard work at Les Sables to make *Crédit* ready for sea, and in this state I had sailed her to Arcachon, where she was put ashore. The keel was taken by road down to the Vendée for radical modifications, and the mast to Lunel to be stripped and rebuilt. It was at this point that the real work began. With the help of my father, who took over the mechanical side, and my friends, we went to work on the hull, and in particular the electronics. I was really glad that my father was masterminding the mechanics. Although these boats are without auxiliary propulsion, the engine is a vital component – without its presence to charge batteries, all the systems so vital to modern ocean racing would be useless. Running out of fuel in one of these boats is as great a disaster as in any motor vessel. Once again, my meticulous marine engineer came into his own, working for two exhausting months in the summer sun.

Meanwhile, I was sweating over the navionics and command station. In one of these boats this looks more like something out of an airliner: autopilots – and note the plural – GPS and other navionics, radio and other communications systems. Yes, I was going to be at the controls, but I suspect few airline pilots have built their own cockpit systems! By the time I was finished I knew the boat's circuitry by heart. One advantage of this, of course, is that having assembled it,

I should be able to repair it at sea. Here again I was indebted to my father, whose advice I had to ask more than once.

By this last stage we were some 60 per cent ready. While waiting in nail-biting suspense for the sponsorship that would permit us to get our mast and keel back, we were able to work on the hull, completing the finer perfectionist touches, as far as we could afford them. It remained simply to reassemble the puzzle that my boat still resembled: and finally, finally, to set out.

• CHAPTER 5 •

Alone in the crowd

By now, we were the principal attraction of the port of Arcachon, or so it seemed. Throughout that summer there was a constant stream of visitors: friends, wellwishers and less wellwishers, they all seemed to gather round the determined band working away like ants on a hull shorn of its keel and mast. I'm certain that on balance it was good for us. There were even some who chipped in with contributions – and many thanks to them! The regional sailing association of Aquitaine sent one of their full-time staff to see what help he could give. I wasn't in a position to pay for any help; a trust had been set up to manage the sponsorship funds, and this paid me a minimum wage and Virginie a half-time salary on which we could live. That solved immediate problems for the time being.

I have spoken before of the tremendous help I received from my father, but there are others who should be mentioned, without whom none of this would have been possible, friends who gave unstintingly of their time and their ideas. Francky, an old pal, and Edouard, Christian, Valérie, Didier, the Hardy brothers... No, the list is too long, but my thanks to you all.

Having said that, I owe a special debt to Thierry Eleure. As a top class boatbuilder, he was involved from the first in the development of singlehanded ocean racing. He has since risen to the pinnacle of his profession; it was he who built Titouan Lamazou's boat, in which he won the first Vendée Globe. More recently he built *Aquitaine Innovation*, Yves Parlier's choice for the 1996 race. It was Thierry who first brought me to the notice of the sailing club at the time when I was messing about with sailboard prototypes on the beach. It can't have been serious boatbuilding to him, but he must have thought I had some ideas in my head because he invited me to come and work with him.

As soon as I had got my hands on Jeantot's boat, I went straight to ask Thierry's advice. I sketched out the modifications I wanted to make and discussed them with him, even before talking about them to the boat's designers. He was down at Bordeaux, working on Parlier's 60-footer, and didn't have much time to spare. Whenever I phoned, despite the demands on his time, he was always pleasant and helpful, and gave me tons of advice.

As the summer progressed and that project came to an end, he gave me yet more of his time, and came to see us every day. He went into deep discussions with my father, two technical types together, over the more highly advanced aspects of the project. I should like him to build my next boat, which I hope will represent the state of tomorrow's art, and then we shall see what I can do with her.

There are non-sailors who think a race is just between skippers. Of course it's not; it's between boats, and inevitably also between sponsors, but behind all this there is an unseen technical army, and it's a battle between them as well.

There is another little realised aspect of these long distance races, and that is the physical side. Sailing a craft of this size singlehanded is physical in the extreme, and if the mind must be alert and informed, so must the body be in spot-on condition. Over the winter of 1995–6 I embarked on a training regime.

The Aquaform Centre at Andernos kindly offered me its facilities, and I worked out in the gym, under professional advice, on a regular basis. It made me feel more confident, as I could sense my fitness growing. I'm told that by the end of the training regime I had doubled my muscle mass; Virginie says she greatly appreciated it! I harboured some doubts as to the side effects of such a crash programme, all the same; I should ideally have taken much longer to reach this peak of fitness. At the same time, I had adopted an athlete's training diet – as far as possible, at least; when I was driving thousands of kilometres in search of a boat, I inevitably slipped back into the old regime of sandwiches and Coke.

Travel by now was a little easier; instead of my old van, Renault had lent me an Espace. I often had to go down to the Vendée to check on progress on the keel and on the quality of the work because, quite simply, it would be essential to my survival down in the Southern Ocean. I went constantly, too, to see the other specialists, and I can only say that I remain tremendously impressed by the sheer quality of their work and the enthusiasm with which they carried it out. It was a good move to go round to the sub-contractors in this way, however much of a nuisance I might have been to them, because once again it meant that I got to know the individual components of my boat intimately, far more so than if I had been a skipper rendered insouciant by the ten million franc budget at his back.

Then it was down to Lunel to follow up and work on the rebuilding of the mast, back again to strip and fair the hull ready for antifouling, on to the riggers to see to the new shrouds I had ordered, which were stronger than the originals. Little by little I was putting myself into my boat. I think perhaps that in this way, when we were at sea, the boat and I could understand each other, even communicate. She would quite literally tell me when she wanted a reef pulled down, or when she could stand more sail. Non-sailors may think I'm exaggerating this last point. I can only invite them to find out for themselves, and then they will understand.

I wanted to leave no detail to chance, even though I could feel myself becoming obsessive. I monopolised our video recorder and worked through every film I could find of the Vendée Globe and of ocean sailing generally. I must have watched some footage fifty times! After all, I was learning. Sometimes I'd re-run a tape and freeze frame at a key point. 'Bloody hell, he's going to broach like that,' I'd say. 'That spinnaker's going to give up on him.' Virginie found it exasperating in the end. Imagine, I'd watched a sequence twenty times, and I'd still shout, 'Look! I missed that! That's how he...' All this was essential preparation, and a formidable store of knowledge for me. It was better than books in that this was at first hand, not someone else's version of what happened. I'm sorry, Virginie, but it really was worth it.

Apart from preparing the boat and myself there was the question of stores; four month's food, clothing and medical supplies. Virginie took charge here, and did superbly. Perhaps we were aided by the fact that an obsolescent boat was less sensitive to the last few kilos of stores, thus I was able to avoid the sci-fi rations adopted by some contestants. Any dehydrated rations I took aboard were strictly as an emergency reserve.

No, I did better than that; eating well is as important psychologically as it is physically. And in any case I'm not an astronaut or an alien; I come from south-west France with its ancient tradition of good living! So alongside my every-day rations we loaded on two dozen bottles of well-chosen wine and a case of half-bottles of champagne to mark the symbolic milestones of the race: the Equator, Good Hope, Cape Leeuwin and so on. Then, of course, there was Christmas to think of, new year, the Horn, the Equator again, and finally my return to Les Sables.

As to my sea clothing, I had ordered a range of equipment, including survival suits, to enable me cope with the various extremes of conditions I would encounter. Virginie organised my 'personal' as opposed to 'deck' clothing, and the various changes I would need were sealed in plastic bags. In the event, the hurried conditions of my departure meant that I was unable to see, or even to list, what was in each packing case. However, a leaking ballast tank during the first few days sorted that out for me; the cases were soaked, and I had to repack each item individually.

It may seem less than obvious to those without deep-sea experience, but simple things like the number of pairs of long johns, socks and so on aboard are a vital factor in determining the comfort or otherwise of a voyage. When ocean sailing, you are so often soaked and without the chance of drying yourself, and diesel is a far higher priority for the generator than for heating. Skippers with the money to do so make up bags of clothing for each week, which are thrown overboard when changed. I couldn't do that, but I took all the changes I could, reckoning also to keep as dry as possible. Not, of course, that it worked out that way.

Nor could we forget that race regulations, and of course the law, insist on survival equipment. Liferaft, flares, SAR beacons, iron rations all had to be packed on board. Then, vitally, water. I like to have a little too much, so I carried 130 litres over and above tank capacity. If all else failed, I had a sea water desalinator. Charts are an equally vital consideration, and apart from the ocean passagemaking charts I had a packet of small-scale landfall sheets. Although there were to be no ports of call I would be passing close to the Cap Verde islands and others, and apart from the necessary information they conveyed, I would be able to dream a little, and see the islands in my mind's eye through the charts. And along with them, there were the inevitable tide tables and nautical almanacs.

For everyday use there were two portable PCs, one set up for satellite communication purposes, which I could use to send faxes, and the other for navigation. Both were linked to my GPS. As a student, I had learned Basic, but was never a computer buff as such. My voyage was to change all that. The computers provided an open window on the world, and became by friends.

As the summer drew to a close, I was still working on the boat in the hot sun, but what brought me out in a sweat even more than the weather conditions was the knowledge that I was still waiting for funds to cover the work on the mast, keel and sails. I was all too aware that they wouldn't be released without payment. It was at this agonising point that Jean-Claude Le Monnier, chair of the Algimouss company, came down to meet me and see the boat. It was the first of a series of meetings which ended in October with my being given the green light at long last. Algimouss would put up a million francs, a third of the budget!

Frantic phone calls to the various contractors followed, to say that their money was on the way. I asked for the earliest possible delivery, for only two weeks remained before the start date. I don't think there can ever have been such a fortnight in the history of ocean racing. Total strangers seemed to turn up from nowhere to help us replace the keel, step the mast and rig it, and get sails and stores aboard. Passing acquaintances brought us beer and sandwiches to save vital minutes of the working day. It was a time of total delerium, with the inexorable countdown in the background to the day I would have to set off on the qualifying race. Our patchwork team seemed to be accomplishing a miracle.

So, finally, the day arrived when the last stores went aboard, and my *Algimouss*, with her new name, seemed to say to me, 'Well, what about it, then?'

• CHAPTER 6 •

The outsider

For my qualifying stage the Vendée Globe organisers had set me a stiff passage: from Arcachon, round the Fastnet, and back again – a matter of two thousand miles or so, which would not have been so bad had it not also been my shakedown passage in a boat which had not yet been to sea after a radical refit. One or two other contestants had been in a similar position, but I was the most pressured of the lot. It was a very far cry from motor racing, where a rebuilt car will be run on a test bed, then given track trials, and perhaps a new engine and wheels before its first race!

I shall never forget my departure from Arcachon after those two weeks of feverish activity; it felt as though it was my big departure for the Vendée Globe, and in a way, it was. In the harbour and on the pontoons an incredible crowd had gathered. Some had been there all night watching our last minute preparations. There were thousands of people there to wish me luck, and I tell you, I was proud. When I set off there was a more intimate farewell from my team; I don't think there was a dry eye amongst us. Then came the cheers and the shouts of 'Good luck!' Those cheers were my best recompense for all those months' work and uncertainty. As I passed down the inner basin, surrounded by a flotilla of small craft, I felt carried along by the shouts of encouragement. 'Thank you, thank you all,' I said to myself, 'I won't let you down.'

At sea, it was another story. Out in the Western approaches it blew force 9, and dead on the nose. Not only was I not gaining any ground, but there was a serious risk that something might carry away. At this rate it was likely to take me three or four days to reach the Fastnet, where an even deeper depression was building up. How I envied the other contestants, who had been able to complete their qualifying stage in summer! Fate seemed to have done the dirty on me; to remain out here, falling into the same hole twice, and just waiting to lose my mast wasn't a qualification, unless for the psychiatric hospital. I decided to put the helm up and return to Les Sables d'Olonne. There was little point in ending my circumnavigation here in the Channel by seeing my dreams whipped away along with my rigging. So it was that I arrived back without having completed the qualifying passage, and I advised the race committee of the fact as quickly as possible; there was little point in lying about it. The race would start in four or five days, and this gave hardly enough time to sort out the few bugs which had surfaced during the shakedown phase. Everyone was there – Virginie, my father, my friends – and they pitched straight into the boat, working like demons.

To add to all this pressure, the crowd was growing by the minute round the harbour and in the cafés: there were other contestants and their support teams, journalists, doom-wishers and Joe Public at large. Meanwhile, the race committee had sent for me and thanked me for the frankness of my report. They would consider it, and wished me good luck. Later in the day they met again, and sent for me. The president spoke:

'We have considered your case; in view of the fact that you returned to Les Sables without having covered the qualifying distance, we regret that we are unable to accept your entry.'

The sky had fallen in on me.

'No-one is going to stop me,' I shouted.

'No-one can stop you sailing the course. But you cannot do so as an official entry. If that is what you decide to do, good luck.'

They were not unsympathetic, but insisted that they had a duty to perform. I tried to appeal to them.

'Please, come and inspect my boat. She is ready in every respect to take part – you won't find a single fault. My sponsor declared late in the day, so I wasn't able to complete my qualifying leg in workable conditions, and I was honest with you about the fact that I'd had to put back. Can't you reconsider?'

They wouldn't come to see the boat. I was furious; they might have at least accorded me that courtesy. The race organisers, with Jeantot presiding, confirmed the committee's decision, but expressed their support should I wish to sail the course.

'As far as I am concerned,' Jeantot declared, 'there are sixteen contestants, not fifteen and an outsider. He's paid an entry fee, he has a race monitoring beacon aboard, and I'm going to include him in all bulletins.'

Over the remaining days before the start, the gossip began. Some took my side, some ran me down, saying how right the race committee had been, that I could hardly expect special dispensation if I wanted to arrive at five days' notice for a world class event, and so on.

Whatever they said, I was still going. I was going to sail the Vendée Globe – that was what counted. I recognised that I needed a few more days' preparation, but there was a solution; I could cross the start line, then put back into port for initial adjustments. That much was provided for in the race regulations; Tony Bullimore was planning to do the same, as was Nandor Fa. Yves Parlier's support team had offered to assist my own outfit if I chose this option. I would lose four days, but would set out again with a boat 100 per cent ready.

And yet, I didn't want to take this course. I was driven on by hatred, and I had got the bit between my teeth.

I knew what the alternative would be, of course; I should have to work and cobble away for weeks singlehanded at sea if I were to have the boat in a fit state to face the Southern Ocean. But I might still have taken the softer and more sensible option if it had not been for one last insult which remained: I was refused entry to the race briefing meeting. I was even threatened that if I sailed within the regulated zone allocated by the marine police to the contestants on the start line, the committee would ask the police to remove me! I took myself off in a thunderous temper. Another contestant showed what he thought of their behaviour by photocopying the sailing instructions and passing them on to me.

When I had calmed down, I decided to start half an hour after the others. I was still pretty livid, however, despite the fact that all the other skippers came to see me and reassured me that as far as they were concerned, I was taking part in every sense of the word. Now, just a few hours before the start I had to calm myself in the face of all that had gone on. Outwardly I managed to remain calm, despite my feelings. 'You're going to do it,' I kept telling myself, 'You're sailing the Vendée Globe!'

I did my best to isolate myself during the last hours, otherwise I think I might have cracked up altogether. Virginie and I managed to get away for an hour or two before the start. We needed to be alone together, so we went down to the boat, now deserted, and went aboard. Little Philippine played around the stowed sails as we said our goodbyes.

As the start time approached, our little one was taken ashore. Virginie stayed on with the rest of the team, who would not leave the boat until the tow was ready to be cast off. It was a fraught time; it wasn't easy to watch the other contestants being towed out of the harbour, and be left alone. When the time came, we were towed out of the harbour in our turn, and I found that the crowds were still waiting all along the quay and the mole. We were cheered all the way down.

It was a moving experience, and I was quite overwhelmed by the contrast between the crowd and the bastards who had insulted and rejected me. Their cheers, their support, seemed to carry me seawards.

Virginie was the first to board the tug. Perhaps it was better that way. One by one, after helping me to hoist sail, the team slipped away. I was alone – and I would remain alone for the next three months.

A further test remained in store for me. I am not by nature a solitary person. I had waited for the other contestants to clear the line, and here I was, completely alone. I had not taken part in the grand massed departure of which I had dreamed. Very well, I would be the outsider, the pirate. And yet I was still part of the fleet, one of sixteen skippers with one goal. Over the line, we were seafarers together.

I didn't know them all personally; I had made the acquaintance of Pete Goss, whom I would get to know far better and in unforeseeable circumstances, before the race, and had looked over his boat. Gerry Roufs, by contrast, was an old pal. We had done two Figaros together, and knew one another well. Like me, he had encountered difficulties with sponsorship for the race, had had a rough time at the hands of the media, and was not sure of taking part until very late in the day – and this in spite of being an outstanding seaman.

When I was searching for a boat, I went up to talk it over with him in Brittany. He had given me a great deal of advice, and we had turned the project over endlessly. Here he was, too. One by one, as they were towed down channel, the other skippers had waved to me. But Gerry had made a different gesture: hand on heart as though to say 'my heart is sailing with you'. Months later, not long after my rescue, he would send me a touching message of condolence.

I knew Catherine Chabaud well, too; she also was an old Figaro contestant. We had always understood one another well. Isabelle Autissier was rather different; for some years she had been one of the big names of ocean racing. She had big sponsors behind her, and all the adulation of the media. I didn't appreciate one bit her advising me not to sail the course after the committee's decision. And yet, before leaving, she had kissed me and wished me good luck. Then there were Marc Thiercelin and Bertrand de Broc, old Figaro hands, great seamen and great guys. Christophe Auguin, former Figaro winner, I knew less well, and had never sailed against him. He was to win this year's race.

Yves Parlier, another friend, came from the same region as myself. I knew and liked his family, and his team weren't like competitors, more like friends. They had offered their help should I need to put back and make last minute modifications to the boat. Later, I came to fully appreciate the qualities of Eric Dumont and Patrick de Radigues, first class skippers both.

Thierry Dubois was of my own generation, but we had not sailed in the same races. I had met him in Madeira, during the two-way Transat, and he had told me that he wanted to sail in the big class as soon as possible. His boat this time was as obsolescent as mine, and he too was on a tight budget, but he had had two years to prepare it for the race. I don't think we approached the challenge in quite the same way. He was hypermotivated, and the race was his only priority. He saw weight as an enemy, and carried no wine – not at a kilo a bottle. He was an outstanding seaman, all the same.

So here we all were, looking seaward, and beyond that – what awaited? Over the line, I had no time to dream. There was vital work to do, not least to the autopilots. There were four, and they all had to be set up. It was time to be up and active.

It was the pilots, in fact, that gave me my first headache.

When I switched them on the main circuit protector tripped, and down they all went. With the helm unattended we bore right away to starboard. My team, watching from their RIB, howled, 'Put back! Put back!' down the radio. There was no question of doing that, however, but I had to work fast – I had no pilot, no power, and there was a gale imminent!

I rigged up my oldest autopilot, a spare, as a temporary measure, but had hardly had time to breathe when the staysail halyard carried away and the hanks jammed on the stay. I had to take insane risks, climbing the shrouds to ride the sail down and hand it; it took me half the night, and by the time the sail was stowed and the halyard re-rove it was blowing force 8 to 9.

I didn't really have the sail wardrobe I needed; I was sailing well off the wind, and unlikely at this rate to weather Cape Finisterre. And the pilots were still down. I called my father up on the radio and told him I was likely to have to put back. 'Don't do that,' he replied, and proceeded to talk me through the circuits. We worked out eventually that there was too much power on the circuit breaker. Under his direction, I separated some of the circuits. We tried again, and this time the pilots worked. It had hardly been an auspicious start.

During these first days, it was a battle against the sea. There was a lot of water slopping about in the bilge, and I didn't have time for as much as a sandwich. Beyond Finisterre, life became quieter. I started listing everything I would have to fix, noting each one on a post-it slip. Soon there were so many that the cockpit seemed full of them. Would I be capable of sorting them all? Did I even have the means to do so?

There wasn't much time for communications. I had one session each evening with the race base station, to whom I would give my position, and they would give me an overall situation report. After these first difficult days, though, I started sending a daily fax to Virginie, and these pages came to represent something like an account of the voyage that followed: the only remaining written account, since my log is 3500 metres down.

• CHAPTER 7 •

Haute couture in mid-Atlantic

• *9 November 1996, 1810 hrs* •

Hello my love – I don't know if you will receive this message. Finally, I've a little time to rest, but I don't feel too buoyant. There's masses of work for me to do here. We're running before the wind, down to the Canaries. The others are under spinnaker or gennaker at present. I've no met information, and as it's the weekend, I don't expect any until Monday!

An incredible amount of work to do on deck – mainly running gear. At this rate, I'll be home three months after the others. Time seems to pass quickly. I feel totally ineffective, and this after all those months of work and the mad rush at the end! At the moment I'm giving the ballast tanks another coat of resin. I really envy that lot out in front of me, not just for being in front, but because they were able to do this sort of work on land. I don't know how I feel – glad because I'm here, or in the pits because it's hellishly hard. I think constantly of you and Little'un. I'd love to have you with me. I can only look forward to a marvellous time on my return. Together. With time to ourselves. Do reply soon. Don't laugh, I can't find the cereals and milk for breakfast.

The keyboard's a pig, the keys stick again and again. I don't know what to suggest except that you keep communications going to the press and the sponsors. It's their event now. I'm tired and pissed off. Love you. Very much.

• *11 November 1996, 1337 hrs* •

Hello my love – work still going slowly. No great change there. I'm still very tired, but that ought to get better. Important! Can you tell me where the hand cream is? I'm getting rope burns. Do send me all your news – don't forget to tell me what Little'un's up to.

• *14 November 1996, 1421 hrs* •

Urgent – ask J-P S what the hand cream is called, and where it's stowed. I can only find a small container, and it's empty. It's important – I need to be able to use my hands.

•*14 November 1996, 2139 hrs* •

Hello darling. A fax arrived from you, but it was illegible. I don't know if you received my last fax, but it's urgent – I need to find the hand cream. Tuesday-Wednesday night was a bastard. We were running past the Canaries. I could just see the loom of Las Palmas, and it reminded me of when I was sailboarding down there. The wind backed to SW at daybreak and has risen to over 40 knots. I just managed to get reefed down in time. It's very difficult without proper met information. I ran down too close to the coast of Mauretania during the night – only a few miles off. I was worried about picking up fishing nets. It was a bit hairy for a while. Not a good night. The third reef luff cringle of the mainsail is torn. I'm not sure how I can repair it, and worse, if it will hold. Very dark nights, and the ballast tanks I thought I'd repaired have started leaking again. It's a bugger. I've been three days trying to dry out the pilot berth cushions, and I thought I'd get a dry night. No such luck. I'm still not happy about the staysail. If I can't furl it down south I'm in trouble – to say nothing of the third reef in the main, and all the rest.

I do need to hear from you as often as you can; it will keep me going. Every day is spent cobbling her up, and finding other things to cobble. Some good news though; I'm running in sight of Catherine Chabaud. It feels better. But then I see her changing a spinnaker – and I've not set mine yet. I'm beginning to wonder why I carried one along with me, it's just more weight! Still, we're making for the Cape Verde islands now, and I've managed to find my wind pilot. Mind you, I've just spent forty minutes on the radio to the guy who supplied the software – there are more bugs in it than a dog's blanket! A big kiss...

• *15 November 1996, 1129 hrs* •

Hello my love. The papers for the Espace are in a grey folder in the black case.

For the past two days it has been a bastard here. The boats up ahead have a leading wind, and Dubois, the last of them, isn't going badly. We four – Chabaud, Goss, Radigues and me – have lost our wind. The computer seems to have gone wrong all morning. I don't seem able to receive. Can you try sending me the position of the three other boats? And your news?...

• *16 November 1996, 1904 hrs* •

My love – no work on deck today – we have a leading wind, 20–25 knots. I'm under main and gennaker, and I've just touched Jeantot's record of 26 knots. At this speed we should be up to the Cape Verde islands tonight. I'm going to reduce sail and alter course a little to give a margin of safety. At last I can relax and just watch her sail. Still a bit depressed, I expect on account of what happened before the start. Even now I haven't got back into my stride. I'm constantly depressed. I need to hear from you tremendously. I hope I'm not going to be like this right through the race, because much more of this and I'll put into the nearest port and fly straight home to you. Do send me news as often as you can. Could you get back to me right now? I'm in front of the fax. Ask my friends if they'll get in touch with me too. It would be a great relief.

(*Later*) I've just been on deck for two hours. The wind has risen to 30 knots. I should have handed the gennaker sooner. I reefed the main just in time. Heavy work, but I got there in the end. Night is falling and I'm making 18 knots on the crests, broad reaching under single reefed main and heavy genoa. I've just managed to have a hot shower in the cockpit to get some of the salt off. Feel better. Love you. Can you get back to me before I look up the chart of the islands?

• *17 November 1996, 1538 hrs* •

Getting impatient now. At 1430 I passed the last of the Cape Verde islands, Fogo. It's volcanic and very impressive. I don't think it was the right decision to work through the islands. Pete Goss passed to the east, and that would have been better. Weather very heavy and humid; drizzle on deck, sweat down below. I can't work with resin on the boom, but the crack doesn't seem to be worsening. As for the rest of the jobs, I've done nothing for the past two days. I feel bloody awful. Yves Parlier has pulled off a fantastic chance. He passed much further to the east than anyone would have thought, and has a leading wind; he and the five other lead boats are shooting away. Not that it matters.

• *18 November 1996, 1837 hrs* •

No more news through of you and Little one. I'm worried. I hope you're OK. Do be careful of the cat with Philippine.

You must be very busy, what with everything, and she's getting more active all the time. Do make sure she doesn't have an accident. I know you're coping magnificently...

Getting along quite well now, but have to be careful of violent squalls. Last night I had to pull down the second reef because of the gusts and it looks as though I shall do the same tonight.

Do keep an eye on the telecommunications bills. If it's more than we expected it's because of the technical problems I've encountered. I'd like to hear from my brother, it's important. Can you ask the Arcachon chandler who sold it how to regulate the barometer? It seems to be reading high. There's so many things I want to say to you, but it would take all night. I miss my little family. Let's hope the worst is behind us. We've earned it...

• *19 November 1996, 1517 hrs* •

My love – I haven't much time; we're in a dirty weather system, squalls showing on the radar. The edge of one squall carried me along, but it picked up to 40 knots, luckily from behind. I had too much sail set. Got to close now, wind getting up again. A bit like Russian roulette...

• *20 November 1996, 0833 hrs* •

Dear love – a very difficult night. No sleep. Still in this weather system; slow to pass through it and pick up the Trades. Still haven't heard the others' positions. Closing now, a squall coming up. Back ASAP.

• *20 November 1996, 2103 hrs* •

Done it! Out of the system, after 36 hours and terrible squalls. Very hairy. Close attention to radar needed. Still sweating horribly. Can't open the forehatch in these conditions, and it's like an oven down below. I've a double reefed main and half the genoa – I don't want to chance the staysail. South-east Trades picked up, 30–35 knots and driving to windward. Dirty sea, but not as bad as Biscay.

Camcorder is ready to go, but I haven't got the LCD for editing. We're 177 miles from the Equator, and ought to cross the line tomorrow. The champagne's ready, but no flowers to throw to Neptune.

I'm running ninth, in front of Chabaud and behind Bertrand de Broc and Eric Dumont. Look after these messages, as I've had no time to write up my log.

•*21 November 1996, 1540 hrs* •

My love – I've just crossed the line. I filmed the passage from north to south on the GPS, and the champagne bottle in our wake. I sprinkled a libation to the boat, too – not a great sacrifice, as it was warm! I've heard Auguin has a television aboard, and watched *Un Indien Dans La Ville* while crossing. Autissier has a Standard M Videophone Satellite link. So have five others. Mind you, Isabelle has a budget of 10 million francs. Mine must be the smallest budget, and this boat has been twice round already.

Very tired, another major problem this morning, a crack in the ballast tank at about the level of the worktop. If I'd not noticed it, it would have fused all the electrics on board within a few hours! I've cut through the worktop only to find that the leak is further up. Shit. I emptied the ballast tank to get to work with some resin, and I've automatically lost speed. Until this she was going quite well. I'm going to give it plenty of time to cure, though. I tell you, I'm fed up to the teeth – one problem after another. And this, going to windward in a 30-knot wind. Not a time for a make and mend. I'm worried about the reef tackles; they look as though they could give way at any moment.

OK, enough whingeing. True, I'm not getting along as

ven years old, on holiday in the Pyrenees. A long way from the Southern Ocean!

ilippine's
st taste of
lt water, at
e early age
seven months,
the port of
rcachon. The
ought of her
d of Virginie
d much to keep
e alive after
y capsize.

PHOTOS: RAPHAEL DINELLI

My sailboarding years taught me a great
deal about sailing in extreme conditions.

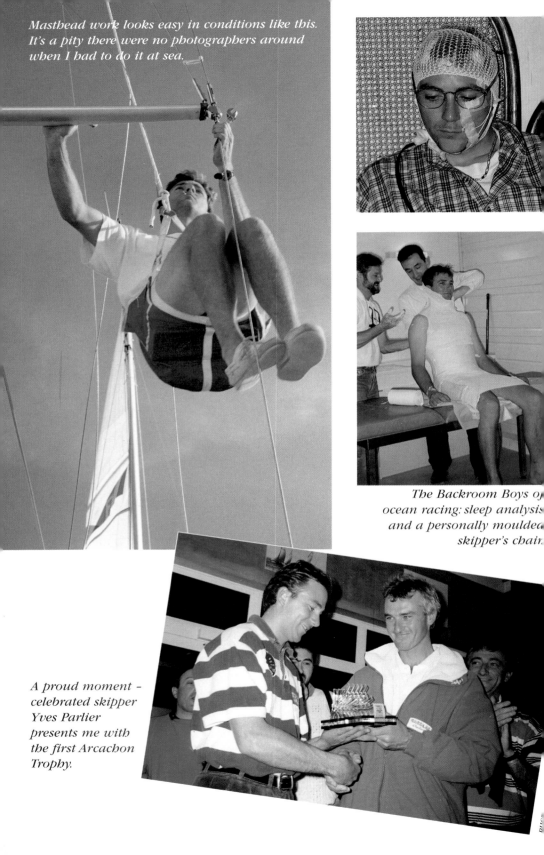

Masthead work looks easy in conditions like this. It's a pity there were no photographers around when I had to do it at sea.

The Backroom Boys of ocean racing: sleep analysis and a personally moulded skipper's chair.

A proud moment – celebrated skipper Yves Parlier presents me with the first Arcachon Trophy.

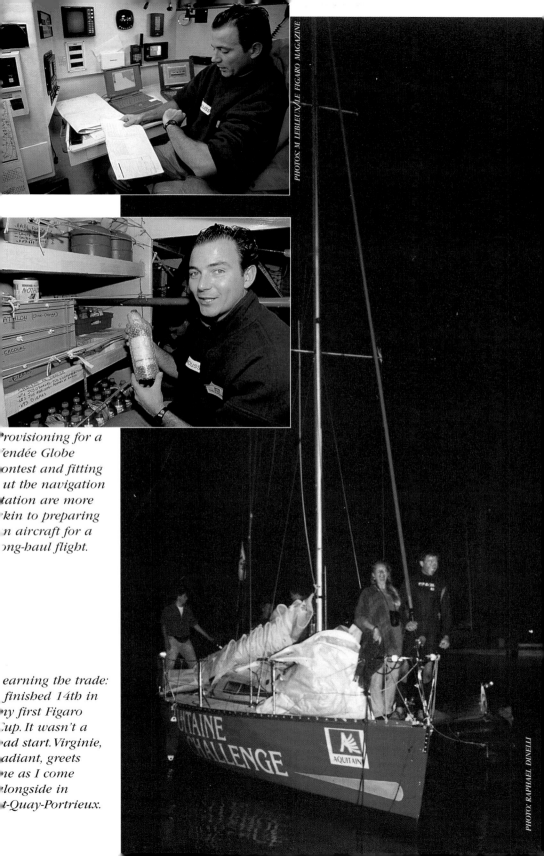

PHOTOS: M LEBLEUX/Æ FIGARO MAGAZINE

Provisioning for a Vendée Globe contest and fitting out the navigation station are more akin to preparing an aircraft for a long-haul flight.

Learning the trade: I finished 14th in my first Figaro Cup. It wasn't a bad start. Virginie, radiant, greets me as I come alongside in St-Quay-Portrieux.

PHOTO: RAPHAEL DINELLI

My father and friends joined me in a mad rush which lasted right up to the last moment to refit Algimouss, *formerly Philippe Jeantot's* Crédit Agricole IV.

It took an old Marine's level-headedness to photograph seas like these, down below the 50th parallel, while sailing to my rescue.

PHOTO: REX FEATURES/SIPA

Before abandoning the liferaft I salvaged the Argos beacons - and my bottle of champagne!

...iday 27 December. I was half dead from cold and exhaustion – but saved! Not too far ...ne, though, to hold up a bottle for Pete, before he hauled me aboard Aqua Quorum. *...e was pretty exhausted too.*

Eyes burnt by the salt, hands frost-bitten – these were the hallmarks of a close encounter with death. For the following 12 days my rescuer would be my doctor.

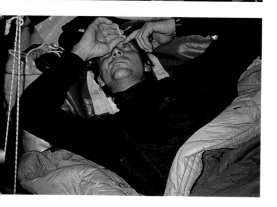

Perhaps not the crown jewels, but without these fantastic Argos beacons I would have been lost.

afely ashore in 'obart. For Pete, >e race was to ontinue.

Above and below: *23 March. Two and a half months after setting me ashore in Hobart, Pete Goss completes his circumnavigation, with a crowd of 100,000 waiting to greet him. Here I was just one of the many.*

Catherine Chabaud enters port amid congratulations all round.

Santé, and here's to friendship!
We enjoy a long-awaited cold beer together in
the Galway Bar, watering-hole of the sailors of Les Sables.

well as the others. And it's not much fun. I hope the boat and the skipper are going to be up to the Southern Ocean. Send me some news, I need cheering up. And tell my father there's a problem with the ballast tank – starboard inlet leaking, and lots of water in the bilges.

• *23 November 1996, 0926 hrs* •

Dear love – Very worried these last few days about the ballast tanks leaking in all directions. There are cracks, and noises which aren't at all reassuring. They could release three tons of water into the boat. The scuttles are leaking, and there are leaks in the bulkheads on both sides where the yard fixed the chainplates. And worse, I can't get at the bastards. I'm in deep shit. Contact Thierry and let me know what he has to say...

•*24 November 1996, 1954 hrs* •

My love, don't worry. Some news for you. Today conditions were good enough to work on deck. I've bent on the stay-sail, but singlehanded on a boat like this it was long and hard – especially getting the sails up out of the locker, and then repairing them. You can't imagine the number of hours I've spent sewing. It was a job to remember, sewing thick Kevlar-polyester sails by hand. It's incredible. It made me think of my grandfather, who was a cobbler. I found I was doing just what he used to do, working with a heavy needle and palm. Just like putting a new sole on a boot! The day went quickly. It's evening now, and I can breathe again. I've been working on the met after receiving my first fax since the Canaries. The south Africans seem to have a good met service.

It seems the anticyclone off St Helena extends a long way south, I'm likely to be becalmed and to have less favourable conditions than the lead boats. Again! Above all I hope not to lose contact with the rest of our group. Firstly, I'm heavier than Chabaud and Goss, and will go less well in light winds. Secondly, though, I'll use the light conditions to work on the leaks rather than pouring over an analysis of the met. It's rather a risk, as good weather tactics in light airs could gain or lose me a hundred miles.

Send me some news today. And tell Christophe that the fax he sent yesterday was terrific. Tell him to write more often. And do send me a long, long fax!

• CHAPTER 8 •

In the hell of the Roaring Forties

• 25 November 1996, 2032 hrs •

My love – It's all go here. The staysail is nearly finished, and I've one reef cringle to sew on the mainsail. I've been up to the hounds for the first time since we started out, to free the staysail halyard. Then, since I was there, I made my way up to the masthead – 26 metres. It's just as well that I did. Intermediate shrouds D3, D4, both sides, were slack, and the internal halyard for the gennaker was just hanging on by a strand or so – nearly chafed through. Now, this evening, I have to cobble up the cuts and other damage I sustained sorting it out. Being 26 metres up with a big sea running wasn't fun. I handed the gennaker, as I was afraid I might lose it overboard. I must raise Hervé tomorrow morning to check the shroud tension. If I have to retension them it's going to be hell on wheels. Whatever happens, I'll be up and down again twice tomorrow for the gennaker halyard alone.

I think I've worked out an anti-chafe system. And I've not even set a spinnaker yet! If I can't get the gennaker up again, I can forget the race. I've heard over the radio that Thiercelin hasn't a halyard left at his masthead. The shrouds could be very problematical. We'll see tomorrow. Going to try to get some rest now. I ache all over.

• *27 November 1996, 0858 hrs* •

Dearest love – A good 25 knot wind this morning. No question of going to the masthead. It may be just as well, as I don't feel on top of the world. I lost the gennaker over the side, and getting it back did for me. It's 150 sq m; nearly as big as the main, and I couldn't heave to for fear of getting it under the keel.

I'm going to have to do some stretching exercises for my back. The met looks bad for the next few days, with a chance of headwinds. When I think the lead boats are already running their easting down... I'm just jogging along here like an old sailing fisherman. Oh, shit. Send me a long letter with all your news. It will sort me out a little.

• *27 November 1996, 2050 hrs* •

My love – so glad to get your message, it's the first all day. I've made a nice all-in soup, just the way I used to with François down at Tarifa. I did some work this morning, then slept till 1300 hours. Then some more sewing. After this soup I'm going to get my head down again. I'm a mass of bruises; my arms are black and blue, hands feel like old pumice stone – not much fun. Not too easy, either, with the basic three days' forecast from Meteo France. It's useless with the MaxSea program needing five days' data to work out a course. All the others have either bought in the extra two days' predictions or are using Meteo Consult. It's not exactly a level playing field. Having the satellite images would help too. I hope tomorrow will be better. A big kiss. Send me a few words back, then I can at least enjoy sweet dreams.

• *28 November 1996, 2021 hrs* •

My love – Your fax was cut off short, but I think I received most of it. The wind has backed into the south, so I'm driving to windward. And now it's fallen flat calm. Very odd, and with this sea running, everything is slatting about. I've lowered sail to avoid damage, and will hoist it again when the wind comes. I'll have to work on the winches tomorrow – they were jammed by the salt.

The inspection hatch in the ballast tank is still leaking, so I tried radical measures – took it off and replaced the seal with one from a pressure cooker. It worked. I'm feeling much better, and have been able to get up to the masthead to replace the gennaker halyard. I always go on about work but this time it was fantastic. From the masthead, there is a sensation of being on top of the world, and feeling its curvature round the horizon. Quite magical. Looking down, it was as if from a helicopter.

The mast has been damaged by chafe; I had to go up again with an angle grinder to relieve the carbon fibre round the sheave hole and smooth it. If I lose the gennaker halyard the way I lost the lower one I won't be able to get up and replace it. If that happens I might as well go home! I've retensioned the intermediate shrouds, which is reassuring. We'll see about the met tomorrow.

Is there any chance of getting Little'un to talk to me over the radio? It would do a lot for me.

• *30 November 1996, 1757 hrs* •

Dearest love – feeling low since yesterday – sick, and I have a headache. Possibly overwork. I'm sleeping well, though.

The weather's no joke. There's a head wind and a cross sea slamming against the hull. I've a double reefed main. It's difficult to choose the best course: continue south-west, or come about and head east? I'll decide tonight. No news at the moment of anyone. Radio reception is very bad in the evenings, but I'll try to raise you with a link call; don't know if I'll get through. I haven't worked on the boat these past two days. Miss you terribly. Will speak to you this evening or tomorrow.

• *1 December 1996, 1917 hrs* •

Dearest love – the end of your fax was missing again. At least is got as far as 'Love y....' Hope you're feeling happier. Perhaps I've been making you feel depressed. Since last night I've been working through the eye of a system. I had to tack twice during the night, and have been beating to windward most of the morning. Slavery. It's worse than the Canaries. Chabaud and Radigues have almost caught me up. I've freed the seized winches, though.

I've had the main down to reinforce the third luff cringle, and just got her up again. It was a pig of a job singlehanded. I've had to stop sewing, though; my right hand is in a bad way. I'll be glad to be out of this anticyclone and pick up a leading wind. Those lead boats are a long way ahead!

Some news of Isabelle. Her starboard rudder has gone, and she's closing the Cape. I think she'll put in for repairs. Try to phone me about 1000 hrs French time and let me know all you can find in the papers. Look forward to tomorrow. Must put about now; hope it goes well. I could do with a good night's sleep.

• *2 December 1996, 2013 hrs* •

Your messages are still being cut short. Have been to the masthead to try to work out the halyard problem. I took a chance and set the gennaker. If the wind doesn't strengthen it'll be OK. We'll see what tomorrow brings. I think I lost a lot of ground today.

• *3 December 1996, 1416 hrs* •

Dearest – not much fun. I've had a huge disappointment: in two days, Chabaud and the others have got 200 miles further ahead. If this continues some bugger is going to lap me! After a month's race, gaining a few miles each day on the others, in spite of all the problems, really felt good. And now

I've lost it again. It's heartbreaking. I'm now feeling the extra weight of the boat, and I can't set the gennaker.

But now I have to make ready for the Southern Ocean. There's lots more work to do, but I feel OK about it. I hope the sponsors do too. Getting caught in that anticyclone didn't help at all. Bertrand de Broc lost two places in the same way. I've had more problems with the boom hitting the coachroof and threatening to wreck it. I don't want deck leaks over the navigation area! With this sea running, I can't do what I'd like to about it. The main thing is to prepare for the south, myself and the boat. See you.

• *3 December 1996, 2115 hrs* •

Dearest love – I've just finished work. Nightfall and tired out after two hours working on the mast. I finished smoothing the sheave hole to stop chafe, but the drill battery ran down, so had no choice but to finish with a rasp. It was hard work. I was fed up with being up there, but I saw Catherine Chabaud and Patrick de Radigues. It was just like an aerial photo – pity I didn't have a camera. I can now set the gennaker again and hope to haul up to them. I finished the repairs to the mainsail too. Not before time – it's been a month's work!

I've just received your fax. Keep cool! I'm going to eat now, and change the dressing on my finger. I think the worst is behind me. Catching up to the others makes me feel better. Till later...

• *4 December 1996, 0755 hrs* •

Sweetie – A very rough night, with constant changes of course. I had two very bad gybes – I thought the battens would carry away. Will try to raise you this evening. I'm ready for breakfast now. Thanks for telling me about Little'un.

• *7 December 1996, 1303 hrs* •

No news for days. You've all forgotten me! I've had more problems with the autopilots. Not too worrying for the moment. The desalinator is US. Will have to contact MT on Monday. Its electronics seem on the blink. I'm not surprised – they have an estimated service life of five years, and this one's seven years old. I had hoped it would be OK after so many hours spent renovating it. Its replacement cost is about 30,000 francs, but for a good reliable one like Gerry Roufs' it's more like 80,000. Who said the best things in life are free? The battery drain is worrying. But I'm into the Roaring Forties! Running my easting down, like Radigues. I think it's a better course than Chabaud and Goss who are further south. Send me some news. Miss you...

• *8 December 1996, 1840 hrs* •

Dearest love – The desalinator is running again, and I've had a hot shower. I even shaved. No work on deck. I haven't been up to do repairs for three days; it's been foul weather. I've made several sail changes though. Another depression is approaching; deeper and bigger. The weather is worsening, proper Forties stuff. I've secured everything, and moved all possible weight aft to keep the bow buoyant. I don't want it digging in, and with *Algimouss* being heavy the trim is important. The exercise will do me good. That's what they say, isn't it? I'm starting to see albatross – some of them are following in my wake. I do like it, it reminds me of the dolphin who leads boats into Arcachon. Perhaps the albatross is the same. Hope he isn't a storm warning.

Funny thing, your fax always seems to arrive while I'm writing one to you. I loved the news of Little'un. Will try to raise you on a link call in a minute. I'm still trying to look after my hands, as they're slow to heal. I have to be careful; small cuts can be serious down here. I'll write tomorrow. Tell Little'un what Dad's doing.

• *9 December 1996, 2048 hrs* •

Dearest love – It's hard work even to write at the moment. I've just finished rigging an autopilot – one out of three. While I was setting it up, it went haywire and we gybed. I ended up flat on the deck with the genoa aback and the main jammed up against the backstay. I thought we were going to lose the mast. All this in 40 knots of wind – scared the arse off me. I don't know how much wind the pilot will stand. It feels as though the wind's rising, too. Why do I always have to reef at night...

• *9 December 1996, 2128 hrs* •

I forgot – Patrick has lost his radar. Not from a breakdown, but torn from its mounts! He's now following in my wake, relying on me to keep radar watch for icebergs for the two of us. He's very pissed off – tells me he hasn't been able to raise anyone beyond VHF range since the start – not his family, nor the race station. What must he think of the jokers who say he must be enjoying the solitude? We are within easy VHF range of one another. Now he can talk to me, and I've relayed his messages to his family and sponsors. He asks if I have any cigarettes. Are there any in my Christmas box? Poor sod, he's a chain smoker, and he's run out. It would be a nice present for him. Can you reply before 0900 hrs tomorrow, French time?

• *10 December 1996, 1939 hrs* •

My love – There's a very heavy sea running, and short and breaking at that. The boat's weaving about, and very difficult to keep on course. Since last night we've had winds of 40 knots, now up to 50 since the afternoon. It was very hard to pull down the third reef – the tackle stuck, and is chafed. It took me an hour, beam on, crests breaking over me, to free the tackle with pliers and a hammer. I hope conditions improve, as the tackle is rubbing on the carbon of the boom, and reefing is hell. I think I must be losing ground as I can't hoist sail again. Don't think I can sort it out for the moment with the wind rising and a black night. I'd risk wrecking something vital or going overboard.

The electronics are still going haywire. It makes things very difficult, as when I'm beating I lose my wind indicator, both direction and strength. I'm having to sail by the seat of my pants, and when she dips her nose and surfs at 20 knots it's not a time to be gybing! The autopilot's holding up well, but with crests breaking over the stern all the time I don't know how much it will stand. I have to close down now, the motion is too violent. It's hell on wheels. I'm wedged in front of the PC to write this. A big kiss.

• CHAPTER 9 •

One capsize after another

• *11 December 1996, 2050 hrs* •

Dearest love – Just a brief word. It's bloody awful here. The wind indicator has seized. We've had four or five gybes during the day – inevitable in the circumstances. I'm afraid of losing the mast. I'm at my wits' end with these constant windshifts. Have you any race news? Must close, motion too violent.

• *15 December 1996, 1936 hrs* •

Dearest love – No news from anyone for a long time. There was lots of work to do today. It's the calm before the next storm, so I made the most of it. One big problem – the collision bulkhead is pulling away from the hull. It's a bastard. I told them at the yard that the repair they schemed out wouldn't be good enough. Jeantot had sprung the bulkhead in the BOC challenge. They carried out a temporary repair, and when I took over the boat I asked the yard to take it out and rebuild it, but they said it would cost too much, so they dried out the old foam and laminated a new outer layer in place.

I don't think it threatens my safety, there are two more watertight bulkheads. But if it comes away I will lose 4 or 5 knots and would have to put into port for repairs. Nothing can be done from the outside. The wind is easing. I'm tired and pissed off. A big kiss. Call you tomorrow.

• *16 December 1996, 1957 hrs* •

Dearest – Nightfall down here is now at 1700 hrs, and daybreak at 0130. Don't send me any more faxes in the evening.

• *17 December 1996, 0716 hrs* •

Dearest love – The nights are getting steadily shorter. It's a funny time zone. Water temperature is down to 3 degrees. Have started a radar watch for icebergs. I'm now using the Forties Special duvet, the one with the Goretex outer.

It's a real pleasure to get below. I'm getting out my polar gear. At nightfall, to keep warm, I close all the outer hatches, then with the engine running to charge the batteries, open the accommodation doors, which warms things up a little. I should have another couple of days before the next depression approaches, so I'm getting on with preparations. Today I got out the storm jib and lashed it down on deck, as I can't reef the staysail properly, and it's too big for heavy weather. I had a job getting it down: with a 50 knot wind right aft and a 5 metre sea running, it was no joke on the foredeck. I'm taking special care. One problem is that I have so much gear lashed down on the foredeck there isn't much room for the storm jib. It looks a bit like a jumble sale up there.

Last night I passed the Crozet islands, and looked them up on the landfall chart. Next waypoint, Kerguelen.

• *18 December 1996, 1022 hrs* •

Dearest love – I have just changed satcom regions. Communications will now be via Italy. Can you confirm if it's working?

Tons of work here yesterday. I got the storm jib ready to go, and went up to re-rig the whole starboard lazy-jack system. Discovered that the radar scanner mount was working loose. Finally I had to glue a length of split hose over the starboard crosstree as chafing gear, because the mainsail was working against it with the wind free. It took a good two hours.

My left arm feels much better now. Had a good night, if a short one. It's the midnight sun effect down here; sunset around 1700 hrs and dawn about midnight. It seems odd to be sleeping by day. I'm not counting the days, but I can see the weeks pass as the ration boxes grow less one by one. You put in three weeks' boxes of 'Forties Specials', but I think it's going to take longer than that. At the start I was eating a little ahead of estimates, but I seem to have found my own rhythm and have managed to keep a supply in hand over and above. Just in case.

Is all OK at home – you're not too tired out after moving house? And Little'un? I just love to hear her on the RT. Do make sure the cat stays outside, won't you? A big kiss. Looking forward to home so much.

• *18 December 1996, 1208 hrs* •

Dearest love – This morning I was relaying some news after a radio chat between we four musketeers – Chabaud, Radigues, Goss and D'Artagnan. Catherine tells me she had a bad fright. She broached, with the mast in the water and her on deck at the foot of the mast. Her long wave set is US, and I passed her some info from my manual; luckily we have the same model. Her radar scanner is US too, so I've been passing info from my radar watch for icebergs.

For my part, the wind is forcing me to pass south of Kerguelen. That's not too good; I would sooner have gone further north. It means I will lose ground to Patrick and Pete. Eric Dumont saw a large iceberg two days ago, just in my present position! All eyes are peeled now! I'm going to have to gybe to pass round the Kerguelens. I always seem to be attracted to islands.

The wind's rising again. I've got my main electronics working again at last, and I'm going to work over all the mechanical systems one more time. The anemometer's a problem – I need to know exactly where the wind is coming from! Still jogging along OK, though, not taking any silly risks. Maybe we're a little undercanvassed, but conditions here can change so fast. I'll give her the gun a bit more when we're round the Horn – if not for the race, then certainly to get back home sooner. Send me a fax. Lots of nice news, please.

• *20 December 1996, 1229 hrs* •

Dearest love – I feel very low. I haven't heard from you, and I'm worried about you. Communications here are very difficult. We had a very bad night. Wind over 50 knots, and down on our beam ends four times. There's a total potmess below, but no damage. At least I've seen what she will do when knocked down. She rights quickly and easily. It's very reassuring.

I feel so low, I'm going to bed. We're still under a third reef and storm jib – not fit to set the staysail. Water temp is down to 1.5 degrees. I'm now more than 50° south; very cold. I'm going to try to work to the north. Send me a long letter – I'll feel better for it.

• *21 December 1996, 1002 hrs* •

Feeling better today. I gained confidence from the boat's behaviour in a knockdown. Urgent: contact Le Monnier and ask him for a good photo for an end of year press release. '*Algimouss* and Raphael Dinelli wish everyone a happy new year for 1997.' It needs to be done now. Send your messages between 0500 and 1600 hrs French time, not later. I'm still relaying Catherine's messages. It's going to be expensive for those link calls.

Better conditions today; wind 25 knots, two reefs and the genoa – much more enjoyable. I did some more work on deck, but my left arm has started playing up again; the tendons seem inflamed. I'm trying to rest it.

Pete Goss has passed ahead of me. He's down at 54° south. Must be mad with all those icebergs.

• *21 December 1996, 1426 hrs* •
Dearest – Your fax not getting through. Not sure why. Night falling here.

• *23 December 1996, 0553 hrs* •
I've worked my way a little further north. It was too cold so far south. Possibly it's a psychological effect: 50° south *feels* cold.

Very fraught day yesterday. I started by hearing a strange noise from the starboard rudder. Looked over, and there was a mark on the antifouling. I managed to lever the blade up, and found a huge raft of wrack caught on the keel and rudder. It must have been trailing a good 20 metres behind us. She felt dead in the water. I used a boathook to free the rudder and furled the genoa. I then put her about a number of times, and finally shook the weed off, but it must have taken a good hour.

More and more chores. Surprise, surprise! I lowered the main and sewed a protective patch on right by the crosstrees. It took me all day to sew on a patch of 20 cm x 10 cm. What a performance! I had to lift up the folds of the main, and then go constantly from one side to the other to force the needle through. The wind got up again, so it wasn't easy to rehoist the main. Radi and Pete must have overtaken me now. After our radio chat I crashed out, absolutely shattered.

The wind's in the north this morning, 30 knots. We're sailing under staysail and double reefed main. It's no fun either, having to go out on deck at night to change sails. It looks like another cold day. I'm looking forward to hearing from you. Nothing received yesterday. A big kiss.

• • •

I was not to read this collection of messages until much later, at home in Andernos. I have to admit they surprised me. I remembered going on about my problems with the boat, but not to that extent about my own problems. Oddly enough it's a time I now remember in a better light despite all its trials. I've heard friends say the same about doing their national service. I realise how hard my whingeings must have been for Virginie, honking on like that.

But then, I suppose, there was a certain amount to whinge about. Financially, the venture was no joke – Pete Goss, for example, had to sell his house to take part – and there was no magic wand to wave that away. I suspect that at the end of days which could be horrendous, I was trying to sink into distant domesticity. I remember particularly tearing the muscle in my arm and wanting to talk about it to Virginie – she was, after all, the only one I could talk to. There were my communications with the race monitoring station and the sponsors, but they were public, and you can't live in public. I enjoyed the daily radio chat between skippers, but it was rather professional, giving distance run and weather conditions and so on. Then, for public consumption, anything I said had to be more positive: certainly, to the media, I was presenting the adventurous side of things. I think that's more the kind of thing I ought to have been saying to Virginie rather than going on about domestic problems.

I ought to stress that there were good times, too, and good times spent communicating with all sorts of people. Apart from talk between ships and discussions through the PC with computer buffs, there were always journalists dropping in for an electronic chat, and of course Jeantot. I enjoyed listening to the other contestants, too; it made me feel I wasn't alone, that others were going through the same trials. And that last aspect is terribly important. I found that being in contact in this way recharged my batteries. It made the isolation seem less. I wasn't forgotten.

Nor will I forget the school at Andernos, who called me up each day around 1500 hrs via the Toulouse comcen. Being on the radio, everyone at sea could hear it: the messages and songs the children sent me. There was one song they sang whose words they had adapted especially for me. It brought tears to my eyes to hear it. The same children, when I eventually came home, sent me messages and drawings and poems.

It was moments like this that made the race part of a more human existence. I loved to think of the children setting their watches to my local time at sea. I hope I was able to create good dreams for them. Perhaps I was living in something of a fantasy world myself, a world of powerful forces, both the forces of nature and forces within myself constantly chasing and stealing up on one another. How could it be otherwise down in that Southern Ocean, when I was experiencing such an incredible place for the first time. This account, this log, ended in a fashion which would live up to this part of the world's reputation – not that I expected it; perhaps I should have. My everyday reference to 'a cold day' in that last fax was to be warmed up in dramatic fashion.

• CHAPTER 10 •

The fatal wave

Christmas Eve. Christmas in the Southern Ocean was always going to be an aspect of this race. Today I think of my loved ones; it will be Philippine's second Christmas; last year, when I was at home, she was too young to understand what was going on. I make up my mind to call home this evening; that means charging the batteries really well, as I shall spend a long time on the radio. While I wait, I send a fax to Virginie:

'Dearest love – There's news coming in from everyone. It's a great pleasure. I'll try to call you around 1700–1800 hrs, after I've opened my presents. I've just realised that with my rushed departure, I didn't leave a present for you or Little'un. So I shall keep your present to me wrapped, and open it when I see you again. We must try to get away for a little holiday together when I return; and then I've thought of lots of things we can do as a family. Will you film Christmas at home for me?

Conditions are difficult here, even for writing. There's a cross sea, breaking violently over the boat. We're still under third reef and staysail. Can you get in touch with me? I'll leave the long wave set on watch.'

Meanwhile, I was glad to be in VHF contact with Catherine, Pete and Patrick. We were still in the same sector, and within easy VHF range, but not exactly close enough to say that we spent Christmas together. So, we joked, we would try to meet up for New Year's Day. It was not to be; Santa Claus was far, far away that Christmas.

The race continued: I was still relaying weather information to Catherine, who was close behind me. During our last radio exchange, I wished her season's greetings, and said I would call again tomorrow, adding that the cold front running ahead of her and behind me did not look too active. Nothing, then, to worry about unduly. Having said that, the wind was right aft, and I knew a gybe was always possible.

Later, however, a radio problem perplexed me more than the difficult conditions. I had promised Virginie and the family that I would call them during dinner, and I couldn't transmit. I spent two hours on the radio without success. I was furious. What a time for communication to break down between me and my loved ones! It was from that point that I began to feel more and more uncomfortable; a sort of intuition, if you like. So it was that my solitary Christmas Eve meal felt less than festive, despite the Grand Cru, the ceps, the foie gras. I tried the radio once more. No luck. I resigned myself to sending a fax.

'Happy Christmas everyone. Radio's down, conditions not the world's best, and we're pitching badly. Not easy to film my Christmas dinner and opening my presents! Just a light Christmas meal, as I have to gybe her round in three hours' time. We should be on the other tack and more comfortable for Christmas Day, then I'll be able to enjoy my special meal, and maybe shoot some nicer film for you all. Thinking of you. Love to all.'

After that I crept into my sleeping bag. It was quite warm. But I still felt that something was wrong. I wasn't sure what, but something all the same. Gradually there came to me the disquieting thought that my cabin, and the berth, were feeling more and more like a coffin.

I turned over in bed, but couldn't sleep. It didn't make sense; there was nothing worrying in the weather bulletins. The sea was getting up, but that was no more than could be expected down here.

Finally – night had fallen – I went up on deck to gybe her round. Generally I don't like to take risks at night, and would sooner heave-to until first light than attempt a tricky manoeuvre. And gybing in these conditions is a tricky manoeuvre. If you get it wrong, the consequences can be serious. It's possible to lose a mast. With these short nights, I could wait for daybreak. It couldn't have been far off.

As I made ready, all seemed well. It was cold, but I was well insulated. Then I realised that the wind was rising. 'That's the cold front on the move,' I said to myself. Just as well that I'd got up. Yes, the front passed. And that's how it began.

The wind started to roar. I reefed down, then reefed again. Three reefs and the staysail, and 40 knots of wind. That front was reactivating itself. 40, 45, 50 knots. I still wasn't too worried, though.

At daybreak there was spindrift everywhere, and the sea was getting worse and worse. I set the storm jib, keeping the deep reefed mainsail, and remained on deck. It was riveting. I shot some film, and still felt that all was going well. The wind was icy, but didn't seem to be strengthening further. This was really something! I took the helm; for a long time since, I had left steering to the autopilot. And for the next hour, I rode her like a sailboard. It was fantastic! I felt on top of the world, surfing on the crests, flying at 20 and 22 knots.

I don't know when I realised my hands were frozen, despite my polar gloves. It was this discovery that made me realise I'd had enough. The wind, which had held steady at 45–50 knots, was now rising. It surprised me, as the barometer hadn't registered a fall. Later, I would hear what had happened. The cold front had become associated with a depression in the south and an anticyclone in the north. In only a few hours, the anticyclone had moved south, and the depression had moved north, effectively squeezing the isobars. It was an exceptional phenomenon.

At this stage I left the helm and went forward to lower the mainsail, which was threatening to carry away. It was a hellishly hard job, and it took a long time to work along the boom, putting extra lashings on. The wind was now at 60 knots, and even the furled sail was trying to balloon out of its tiers. Happy Christmas! This done, I shot a few metres of film of the sea conditions, which were incredible. The wind had risen to 70 knots, hurricane force. Everything was white, with visibility eventually zero. I went below, with the boat surfing on a crest. I looked at the speed on the GPS indicator – 18–19 knots. Where would it all end?

It ended there and then: we broached. And beyond our beam ends, with the mast in the water. Everything went flying. Shit, I'd forgotten to secure the drawers. Away went my spices and herbs from the galley. I remember it well, being knocked down in the Devil's own sea and a 70 knot wind, and I was livid about my galley stores! That good old boat, though; she staggered upright fairly quickly. It had been hairy, but I didn't feel too bad. It was a mess everywhere, so I gingerly set to straightening things out again, when I went flying across the cabin. She was knocked down again.

I felt as if I'd been kicked by a giant. *Algimouss* was righting herself again, and I picked myself up, even more angry about my kitchen stores splattered about the cabin. It would have to wait. I got my foul weather gear on, hooked on and made my way on deck. On all fours. If the boat was overwhelmed at this point I could be wrenched off into the sea. I crawled to the storm jib to lower and smother it. All around were giant breaking seas. It was blowing 75 knots in the gusts. Apocalyptic conditions.

I think, compared with the others who were further south, that I caught the worst of this storm. As the isobars closed in and the wind rose, the sea got up, mountainous and breaking, and far worse, it was short. To think I'd groused about the seas in the Indian Ocean! Patrick and I had both had a rough time there, and been very glad indeed to get out of it. But here I was, reorientating my chart. Half way there, and my big Antarctic chart, which wouldn't fit the chart table, needed to be folded to show the second leg! Despite the conditions, I was elated. On to Cape Horn and home!

Then it was to work again, and in really foul conditions. With the storm jib down – and that wasn't easy to achieve – I went below again to send a fax to Meteo France to ask if they could shed any light on the situation. Although I'm no weather expert, I knew these conditions were exceptional, and more important, I needed to know if they were going to last. It seems this fax was never received. I then sent the same message to the race monitoring centre, and also to Virginie. I was not to know that it was to be the last message from *Algimouss*.

'Wind over 60 knots and gusting to 70. Knocked down twice. On beam ends some minutes. Much damage, chaos below. Mast OK. Self OK but have bruised right leg. Will send more info later. Spray everywhere. 18 knots under bare poles and heeling as if under sail.'

It was 0646 hrs GMT and Christmas Day! I wedged myself in at the chart table to think things through. I had to make a very quick decision, as the situation was serious.

There are classic solutions: lying head to wind, using sea anchors, lying a-hull – but which? I decided it was impossible to bring her head to wind, and that sea anchors would have to be streamed aft. I had two, both for boats of greater displacement than *Algimouss*, which was an advantage. But as I considered how I was going to deploy them, I felt

Algimouss lift to a wave – and this one was no ordinary greybeard.

Waves run in series, and in each series, there is always one that is biggest; the Seventh Wave of childhood folklore. Not that the big one is always the seventh, nor has science ever explained why it happens. This is the wave that hit *Algimouss*: I couldn't see it coming, being below, and I suspect there were problems with the electronics of my speed indicator. But the GPS indicator gave 26 knots. Then 30. Thirty knots under bare poles! It was unbelievable, and I knew it was much, much too fast.

Then we fell, as if in a lift whose cables had been cut. I braced myself as we broached to port, then inverted as quickly, it seemed, as a tossed pancake. The boat hit the trough with a terrible shock such as I had never experienced before. I don't think I realised for an instant what had happened, it was all so fast.

From where I had wedged myself in my seat, I fell towards the deckhead. In fact I was still in the seat, which had torn from its mountings. It was, I think, some seconds before I came to myself, but I don't actually remember any sensation of fear at that moment. I didn't think of being killed. My first thought, I believe, was: 'That's the end of the race for me, then!' Here I was, in an upturned boat in a hurricane, and my race was over. I hadn't felt this way about the preceding capsizes, but now the evidence was all around me. The chart table and computers had torn from their mountings, and lay shattered on the deckhead beside me. Yes, my race was over for sure.

• CHAPTER 11 •

Liferaft adrift!

Gradually – surprisingly gradually – the instinct for survival took over. My race might be finished, but I wasn't going to be. Checking myself over for damage, I was surprised to find nothing serious. And looking about me, I was not facing rising water. So there was time for me to act. First things first: I climbed into a survival suit, collected the SAR beacons and put some emergency food supplies into watertight bags. This done, I was able to take stock of the situation. It wasn't too encouraging.

There were six watertight bulkheads, but the three main ones had failed and were letting water in. The scuttles had cracked from the impact when we fell off that sea, and above all there was the mast to deal with. We were dismasted, certainly, but it had been retained by the shrouds, had punched a hole through the deck, and was beginning to batter its way through the bilges. The water was not rising too fast as yet, and I was able to pass from one compartment to another through the watertight hatches. Going forward to where the mast had come through I found water up to my knees: just as well I had put on the survival suit.

The situation was dramatic, and yet I was surprised to find myself able to admire the transparency of the sea as it broke over the scuttles. The scene can only be described as terrible but magnificent: lying in the trough of a 15 metre sea, it seemed as if I was cocooned, and looking through the underwater window of the finest swimming pool in the world! It was extraordinary: the water must have been down to 2 degrees, the wind was whipping spray everywhere, and yet from where I was situated the clarity of the water seemed to impart some mystic sense of security. People may think that I must have suffered a blow on the head, but I felt quite lucid at the time.

Forward, I saw the mast. It was swaying in the swell, but held captive by the shrouds, which had a breaking strain of 11 tonnes; it would not free itself. As it swayed, it was working like a piston, opening its own hole, tearing at the bulkhead, tearing at the hull. There were terrible crunches and cracks from the carbon fibre, and the water was rising inexorably. The sail hatch had simply been blown in, leaving a 1.5 metre hole.

The situation was horrendous. The three main watertight compartments, including the main accommodation cell, were watertight no longer. The aft compartment, from which I had collected the beacons, iron rations and other survival equipment, was half full of water. When we hit, the supply chests which I had lashed in place had crashed free, smashing into the steering gland and driving it through the skin. I collected as much in the way of supplies as I could, and closed the hatch as I left, knowing I would not be able to re-enter the compartment.

Returning to the cabin, I discovered the water rising there too. I think at this point, shock set in: I seemed to become passive, looking through the still-open watertight hatch at the broken mast, sawing and punching away, holding the boat on her beam ends. It MUST break away! The two Argos SAR beacons which I had switched on seemed not to be working, or so I thought; I imagined it was on account of being inside a carbon fibre hull.

The cold was growing worse; I felt a deadly lassitude. For the first time I thought of death: the whole venture was turning into a catastrophe. And to think it was still Christmas Day in France! I felt sick, it was cold, and the cabin stank of leaking diesel. Suddenly I was sick, violently sick. The end seemed in sight.

Surely, I found myself thinking, the boat should right herself now that the mast was partly down? I had discussed this several times with her designer, Marc Lombart, and he had been quite insistent on the point. Some three hours must have passed since we broached. Then, as I watched, I saw the mast change angle and begin to slide out through the hole it had made! It seemed to free the boat, which began to ride more naturally, to turn, and finally to come upright! I felt like a piece of washing in a machine, finishing up with my face in the rising bilge water, but it was better, much better: I could move again.

Climbing on deck, I cleared away the liferaft ready for launching, but didn't inflate it yet with this tremendous sea running, still a good 10–15 metres from trough to crest. I had hooked on, which was just as well; with so much water in the bilge *Algimouss* was riding low and sluggishly, and was swept by every crest as it passed, throwing me against the winch each time. I could not deploy the raft in these conditions as it would simply be carried away by the wind, which was still howling like a thing demented. What I could do was to make it ready, and so I lashed my watertight bags to it, switched on another EPIRB, fixing it in position on the pushpit rail, and strapping a third to myself so that I could see that it was working. It was the only distress signal I could send, and it had to be sent now.

The boat was settling by the stern. The sail locker filled frighteningly fast, the engine and bilge pumps were underwater, and I couldn't free the mast which was still bashing alongside. The tools had gone: they were somewhere in the flooded midden below. Taking stock, it was well and truly time to call for help: here I was, 2500 miles from the Australian coast, and any seaman can tell when he is in command of the situation or when at the mercy of the elements. There was no doubt which of the two situations applied to me.

The time for whingeing was over. I was fighting for my life, and I suspect I felt that if I was making an effort I could improve the situation automatically: and so it was that I spent the rest of that hellish day attempting to bail out the sail locker with a bucket. I might as well have tried it with a spoon. It probably raised my body temperature a little, but that was all.

Now that night was falling I decided to deploy the liferaft, ready for what the night might bring. I lashed it on our lee side, using the trailing ends of the sheets as well as the raft's own painter. Then I retreated below, onto the galley work-top. It was freezing, and at this point I realised miserably that I had neither eaten nor drunk that day.

With odds and ends of cloth, I tried in vain to stop the leaks on every side. Curled up in a foetal position, I could see the water rising, but the thought of going out on deck was beyond imagination. Here at least I was out of the wind and not yet underwater! I guessed there was a metre and a half in the bilge, with the floorboards floating like rafts everywhere. The boat was constantly being swept by heavy seas, and here at least I had a little protection for the time being. I wondered for how long: I could feel the way the boat shook as each sea hit her. What was best now, to stay here or go for the raft? Either was a dangerous option. It was no easy dicision.

Meanwhile, the water was still rising: I was reminded of submarine crews in those old war films. There was perhaps 50 centimetres of airspace left between water and deckhead, and I was forced into one acrobatic posture after another to keep clear of it. In the end my position became untenable: I was underwater half the time, breathing when the surge would let me. It was time to go. It was still dark, and there was a heavy swell running.

On deck I could see the pitiful state of the boat. Only the two fore compartments seemed to be holding up. I was forced to hang on for dear life. She was settling by the stern: the cockpit fittings and the boom had been torn away, the pulpit twisted as if by a mad sculptor. Knowing the sheer strength of the fittings that had been swept away gave me a sobering notion of the sort of forces which had done it.

When I looked at the liferaft, I saw to my horror that it was floating well enough, but some 30 metres away. It wasn't possible: and yet it was drifting further away – 40, 50 metres. It must have been its natural windage that was doing it, and in that raft was my only means of survival. Flares, water, iron rations, all drifing away from me. Despair. Total despair.

As I watched, a crest picked me up and hurled me along the deck and into the flooded sail locker, striking my face on the hatchway. Then my survival suit took over, lifting me out of the flooded hatchway to the deck again. I tell you, I was lucky: not only to be alive, but not to have ripped the survival suit on the broken carbon fibre, nor to have torn my exposed hands or face on it.

Now, back on deck, I had to face the successive seas that swept us: it seemed that my only chance was to find a foothold, and face them upright. I couldn't see the seas rolling up on me, but I could hear them, so I turned to face them as if I was surfing, bending forward to them and anticipating the shock as they burst over me. I found myself forced to my knees, and remained there, as it seemed to be a better position. The crests broke over me constantly, choking me. But it was the only way. It was exhausting, and I kept snagging my feet in the shrouds, which I had been unable to cut. I was afraid of breaking an ankle or going into another hole in the deck. I could feel I had wrenched one ankle brutally, several times: and yet it continued to hold out.

It was terrible, and it just seemed to go on and on. Each wave that struck me choked and froze, working down inside my suit. I could feel my feet locking up with the cold. I started dancing on the flooded, swept deck to keep my circulation going. I must have seemed like a madman, that black night, in the midst of a raging sea. Perhaps that madness kept me alive. I knew I had to keep moving if I was to survive. Keep moving, moving, moving my legs. And so it went on.

Finally it was dawn. The cold front had passed; the wind had eased to some 45 knots. As the sun got up, visibility was good. The sea was still rough, but not like the previous day. Relatively, it was the calm after the storm. Now the nerve-wracking wait began. I considered the situation: even though *Algimouss* was still afloat, daylight revealed the terrible destruction the sea had wrought, and was continuing to wreak. Only the fore compartment and perhaps one or two smaller ones were preventing her from going down. Just one really bad sea could complete the job. The deck was awash, and so was I, and I could believe the sea temperature of just 2 degrees.

Then there was the question of the beacons. One was strapped to my chest. I had been so long crouched down like an old man that I wasn't sure if I could get up again. Crouched like this, was my body getting in the way of the signal? In the dark, I had been able to see the continual re-assuring flash of the beacon's telltale LCD. With the coming of day, it wasn't too clear whether it was working or not. The other two, fixed to the pushpit, were constantly dipping under. Were they working or not? My eyes were burning with the salt, and I had to shield them with my hand to see whether the telltales were flashing. I tried shifting the beacon strapped to me to make it more effective; but how could I tell?

Physically, I was at the end of my reserves. I could no longer feel my hands and feet, nor look at the horizon. My throat was burning with salt and thirst, and a little traitor voice was repeating, 'She's going down bit by bit, and you can't hold on forever.'

Supposing the beacons were working, what were my chances? Forcing myself to remain rational, I considered the nearest other skippers. It was all guesswork, as I was without instruments, but Catherine was too far away at 300 miles. She couldn't arrive before nightfall, and the next night didn't bear thinking about. If I lasted the day, it would be a miracle. Pete Goss? Too far south, and he would have to beat against wind and current. Impossible.

Nearest to me was Patrick de Radigues. I knew he had electrical problems, and if he wasn't up with me by midday, it would be because he hadn't picked up my signal. I found myself raving out loud, 'Patrick, where the hell are you?' As if he could hear me.

Then there was the possibility of aircraft. But I didn't hold out any great hope. Supposing they had scrambled, I was 2500 kilometres away, too far for a chopper. What might an aircraft be able to do? Could they drop me a liferaft? That was my very last chance. And if that happened, it would be because nothing else and no-one else could save me.

So there I was, at the end, perhaps, of my life. I was half-dead in any case. I found myself talking to my boat: 'Come on, old girl, keep up, keep up; don't let me down.' And I believe she may just have listened to me. She was mortally wounded, but she listened to me.

Little by little, the sea was easing. It was now the best part of forty-eight hours since I had hooked on and gone on deck. I could feel a growing lassitude, and a sense of injustice. Not, I think, against the sea or the boat, but against the bastards back in France who would shake their heads and say, 'I told him so.'

I could feel myself not far from death. I could feel its presence. I felt I had passed the first threshold of descent,

beyond which would lie clinical death, beyond which –
what? I knew I had passed that first threshold. It's that
knowledge which led me to say, much later, that I had
returned from the kingdom of the dead.

• CHAPTER 12 •

Out of the depths,
a bottle of champagne!

Death was lying alongside, waiting. I knew that if I wasn't found within two or three hours, I was done for. In conditions like these, how long would it last – seconds, a minute at the outside? I was no longer afraid. I think I felt that what I was going through was worse. And yet something inside me carried on resisting. I was still thinking of Virginie, Philippine, family, friends. And that I was not going to give up having staked so much on this venture. Not that the sea would give me any benefit of the doubt for that. It doesn't.

Physically, I was at my utmost limits. I wanted to lie down on the deck and sleep. And if I did, it would be the end of me. Bugger it, I would sleep on my feet! I don't know whether I did or not, but some time certainly seemed to pass in a kind of dream state. I knew that was dangerous: I had to keep my head clear. I started to talk to the boat again, and when I felt myself going to sleep, I would whack myself round the face to keep awake. I don't think this lasted long, as the boat turned a little, and a sudden lurch dropped me into the flooded cockpit. It was a brutal but vital awakening.

I had passed the stage of physical pain, but I was hellishly hungry and thirsty. It was forty-eight hours since I'd swallowed anything, after all. In an hour, it would be nightfall again. I'd so counted on Patrick, and he hadn't come. It was very near the end: the boat was going down, and the night would finish things off. I was very near the end of hope, too. I found myself sitting down, head sunk low, when I heard it. A noise. An aircraft.

I raised my head, and stood up slowly. No aircraft in sight. Was I hearing things? Then I saw it. A plane. Something rekindled inside me. I was puzzled: what would he do now? I couldn't see him, but I could hear him turning. He made five or six runs over me like this. What the hell was it all about? I knew he couldn't winch me aboard – so what, then? I began to wave like a madman; and there came an answer. The plane passed over again, and again, and this time they dropped smoke floats, marking my position. These were real professionals: I was at the centre of a square of four markers. What was going to happen now, considering they couldn't winch me up?

The sea had eased enough for me to stand up and watch the show. The plane passed over again, and there it was in front of my eyes; a liferaft, which inflated as it fell. It was like something out of a James Bond film, I thought. I could see long floating lines trailing from it. The plane passed again, and a second raft was thrown out.

Not only had the Australians dropped these rafts close to windward, but with the direction of drift of their trailing life-lines, I couldn't miss them. Good on you, cobbers! I had no difficulty in retrieving the line; the only problem now, in my weakened state, was hauling in a raft and boarding it. All the same, I was surprised at myself: a few minutes earlier, I had felt virtually incapable of movement. In fact I could hardly believe what I was doing: I still couldn't feel my feet, but I was standing upright, with my eyes wide open, and hauling on a line!

Rope in hand, I inched my way aft, although here I was chest deep in water. Every sea flooded over me, but still I started to haul in on the rope. The nearer raft was now downwind, so that I was forced to haul against the force of the wind and waves. The only way I could make progress was to take a turn on the pushpit rail as each sea passed. The raft would snub powerfully, then the line would slacken momentarily, and I would gather in a couple of metres and catch a turn again as the next sea surged towards the raft. It's easy to explain now: then, it took me a quarter of an hour to get it closer.

All this time, like a guardian angel, the aircraft circled above me. I had nearly hauled in, but losing my liferaft once before had left its mark. In particular I was afraid that it might tear against some sharp edge of the broken hull or rig. Hauling in again, I brought the second raft within range as well. I was still chest deep in water, and to make fast I had to remove my gloves. I was afraid that in so doing my hands would be incapable of controlled movement; my feet had lost all feeling long ago. But they didn't let me down, and finally the job was done. It remained simply for me to climb aboard. I was nearly spent, and how I found the energy to do it, I still do not know: but finally, I was there.

Looking around me, I felt a bitter pang of disappointment. No, it was worse than that in my exhausted state. Where I had expected to find an emergency pack with at least drinking water, there was nothing: nothing more than an ASR knife, two sea anchors and a sponge! What I did not know, and would only learn later in Australia, was that everything I needed was in fact aboard. This message was marked on the raft where I climbed aboard, but I hadn't taken it in. It seemed that there was in fact water and food in the floats which supported the lifeline. I had actually laid hands on these containers, and hadn't realised what was in them!

So there I was – safe, but in a bad way mentally and physically. I could feel the salt burning my lips and mouth. I decided to try to reboard *Algimouss* for my bag of emergency rations. The aircraft was still above me, though, and I tried to signal, pointing to my mouth. That language seemed international enough, and they evidently understood, if not then, when they saw me go back aboard. I had to act quickly: the bag was in the lazarette, and *Algimouss* lay quiet in the trough of a sea. I hauled open a hatch, only to have the next sea slam it against my arm. In the end, I caught hold of a loose lashing, and held it open that way. Once again, no gloves, and how cold it was!

There wasn't a second to lose: I could feel her going. The hatch was a tight squeeze in my suit, and I didn't take the chance of going right in: even in the state I was in I knew that would be lethal. Remembering how the lazarette stowage was laid out I felt with my feet – although there was no sensation in them – for the cases ranged round the sides, and prised one loose from its shock cord. It floated to the surface: there would be six or seven small one-meal containers inside. No water, though: and then it occurred to me that the density of water is such that bottles, when submerged, wouldn't float to the surface. Well, that meant I could do nothing about it, and there was no time.

Carrying the small box, I crawled to the guardrail to re-board the raft. Pulling it closer, I tipped the case aboard. This was the last contact I had with my ship: I was abandoning. It wasn't an easy moment. I looked back to say goodbye, and as I did so, a sea swept the lazarette hatch, swirling a bottle, and a champagne bottle at that, out of the hatch and into my reach! I grabbed and caught hold. It wasn't even one of my precious supply of half-bottles but a full-sized one, and thus some unknown person's present, left for me to find. I still cannot understand how it floated, though. Nevertheless – water into wine, or at least wine from the water. A miracle, perhaps: but I held the miracle in my hands, and carried it with me as I scrambled into the raft.

• CHAPTER 13 •

Albatross attack

The heartbreaking moment had come. I made certain the second raft was moored to the first, took the knife, and cut myself adrift. We seemed to slip away fast, very fast. And I hadn't even said goodbye to *Algimouss*. I felt very ashamed of that after the way she had kept me alive against all odds. Within a minute or so, I could no longer see her. I don't know how long she took to go down, but I imagine my opening the lazarette hatch must have hastened the process.

Now, the matter of survival. The aircraft passed over again, and dropped two containers: they must have realised that I was without supplies. They were real professionals: the containers fell very close to me. At sea, though, nothing is that easy. I had no paddles, after all. The only way to reach the manna was to put my mitts back on, and paddle like a demented dog. Finally I managed to get alongside the first container, marked 'water'. It had broken up on impact. The water was gone, but I found a radio, and a message which I was to read later.

To the second pack, then. More frenzied paddling, and I got up to two metres from the thing, when a gust carried it away. The bastard! By this time I was exhausted, and having trouble breathing. I had reached the end of my ability to keep going. I collapsed on the air chamber. My guardian angel had not quite finished with me, though: as I lay panting, some of the debris from the first container floated almost under my nose, among it a cereal bar. Incredible – and it was one of my favourites, too; toffee muesli with raisins. I grabbed it for all I was worth. I'd expected military ration packs, and here was something that Virginie herself might have put aboard! In my disorientated state, I found myself wondering how she had been able to get to Australia so quickly.

I returned to hard reality: my gloves were full of water and ice, so I emptied and squeezed them out. My survival suit was full of water too, and leaking everywhere. I sponged out the raft as well as I could before closing the canopy for the night. Finally, I opened the watertight bag and read the message which had been dropped to me.

'Pete Goss 10 hours south.'

Ten hours? The mad Brit – that means he must have beaten to windward for 150 miles, and against these conditions! It confirmed my guess that Catherine was too far away and that Patrick had problems. And Pete had turned to windward to face that lot? Mad, fantastic lunatic! He could still come unstuck, though: and then how many days might rescue take? Could I survive days more, come to that, in these conditions? I was already experiencing hellish cramps, and could hardly move with the cold.

Painfully – very painfully – I removed the survival suit and poured and squeezed what water I could out of it. There seemed to be a great deal. My cramps were replaced by demented trembling and chattering teeth as I squeezed out the polar suit I wore under it, then put it on again, followed by the survival suit. It wasn't dry, but it was less sopping wet.

My tasks were not over, however. Now it was the turn of the Argos beacons from the boat. I didn't want to keep them all inside the raft, as I wasn't sure what that would do to the signal. One could stay inside, where it was certainly safe. That left the two others. I was concerned about interference, so I didn't want to place them too close to one another. Perhaps if I put them as far apart as possible... so again it was gloves off, a sea anchor out as the wind was rising again, and lash the beacons in place at opposite sides of the raft. It seemed to take a long time. Now perhaps I could eat and drink?

But first, I had to close the canopy again. I looked outside, and there was an extraordinary sight – an albatross, and another, perhaps its mate. So I had company. I had seen them in flight a number of times, but this was the first time one had landed so close to me. I was impressed by its sheer size. They are simply enormous birds. And what a beak – like a great chisel, with a hooked tip. I hoped they would bring me luck, as superstition would have it.

When I first saw the albatross, as I entered the Southern Ocean, I told Virginie about it in a fax. It reminded me of the dolphin of the Arcachon basin. The swatchways of the basin aren't easy, especially in bad weather, and often a dolphin would seem to be leading me towards the open sea. There, he would disappear. It's happened often. It happened when I sailed with *Algimouss* from Arcachon to join the race, and I thought it a good omen. I remembered it each time I saw an albatross flying above me. Many other Southern Ocean voyagers, such as Moitessier, have said the same thing; an albatross can follow a ship for a good week. So seeing these two close to my raft I felt reassured. I was not alone.

That comforting feeling was not to last. The two thugs of birds attacked my sea anchor, furiously. I raved and shouted at them. I splashed at them, as if that would discourage these storm travellers! Did they think it was a fish? I'd never seen a fish swimming close to the surface in these latitudes, but I supposed that the albatross had to eat something. Well, the buggers weren't going to eat my sea anchor, that was for sure, because my safety depended on it.

They closed in on the raft, then, and started to attack one of the beacons, chewing at the aerial! Couldn't the bloody fools taste it was plastic! I tried psychology – the psychology of a lion tamer. I put a gloved hand outside the canopy to distract them. One of them approached to within a foot – but then what? What if they attacked the raft and pierced it? I looked to make sure the second raft was still moored to the one I was in. I couldn't fight an albatross, much less wring its neck – I no longer had the strength. He was more likely to be the winner. I closed the canopy, and flopped down on the raft floor.

There was a sharp crack. For a moment I was terrified that a beak had gone through the raft. Then another crack, and another. This little game continued for upwards of an hour. Then it ceased. Opening the cover, I saw that they were now some twenty metres off. That was good enough for me. I closed up again, exhausted. I was shivering once again, and the cramps had recommenced. It was agonising. All I could do was wait and think of the arrival of Pete Goss in the morning.

And what a night it was. I had gathered some bits of packing case from the supplies that had been dropped to me, and with these I tried to insulate the floor beneath me as best I could. The wind was rising, and the sea was getting up again. Crests broke against the raft, and sent it flying. I could hear them coming, and when they broke it felt as if I was a piece of washing whirling round in a machine. My main fear was capsize: in the state I was in, it would be the end for me; there would be no possibility of righting the raft.

There was nothing I could do about that, though; what I could do was eat and drink. It would recharge my batteries a little. There was no starched tablecloth, not even silver cutlery: just the Australian parachute knife, with a rounded tip instead of a point, which I could use as a spoon. I opened a pack: chicken lasagne. 'Keep chilled,' it said. I could guarantee that! Taking a mouthful was agony, though.

My lips had cracked due to the salt. 'Let's try drinking first, then,' I thought. I reached for the champagne and opened it. It was like turning on a fire extinguisher – the movements of the raft had acted as a giant cocktail shaker. I sipped – and spat. The sparkling wine burnt my lips and mouth. What now? I couldn't waste the wine, but you can't force a champagne cork back into the bottle... I don't know how long I worked at it with the knife to be able to reinsert it.

I tried again to eat. The lasagne was quite salty, which can't have helped. What about trying the muesli bar? And it worked. It stung, still, but I could bite and chew and swallow. Encouraged, I tried the champagne again, and this time I was able to drink. Well, I certainly had my survival to toast! I suspect, in those conditions, it made me more than a shade drunk; I certainly remember feeling lightheaded. I recorked the precious bottle, and tried the lasagne again. It made me feel much, much better. I wedged the bottle into the plastic box containing the food, tucked it between the side of the raft and myself, and lay down.

• CHAPTER 14 •

And now, a cup of tea...

Ithink that third night was by far the longest. I shivered constantly, teeth chattering, and dozed but feared to sleep. I felt that if I did, I might not reawaken. I'm sure that the awful sensation of waiting helped me not to fall asleep, as did the sheer discomfort – the mere word doesn't do justice to the reality – of a liferaft. I felt terrible: I think my mind remained clear, but I'm not sure. Nights are short in the Antarctic 'summer', but this one seemed long enough. When I finally looked outside, dawn was breaking; the darkness had lasted four hours.

By the time the light was properly up, there was still no sign of Pete, but there, once again, was the sound of an aircraft. What was going on? I'd expected a boat, and here was that plane again. It helped enormously, though; once more I felt in contact with the outside world, not forgotten.

Rising to my knees, I waved to them so they could see I was still alive, then tried the radio they had dropped to me. I tried to raise Pete, but got no reply. Then, puzzled, I watched as the plane carried out a similar manoeuvre to the previous day's, dropping smoke floats around me. I imagined that Pete had had problems, and they were going to make another food drop to me. Christ, I thought, this could mean that I'm going to be stuck in this raft for another three, maybe four days. Please, no! It wasn't possible! Then, oddly, I found myself giggling like an idiot. 'If they're dropping food as good as that muesli bar, whatever treats will they drop me for New Year's Eve?' I think I imagined Virginie had a hand in it somewhere.

Then I turned my head – and there was a yellow hull! It was Pete, a matter of 100 metres away. I could see him clearly. The smoke floats must have been intended to mark my position for him. He was to explain to me much later that he had been close by me right through the night, but without being able to see me. He must have taken crazy risks to close me before nightfall, and then after all that, couldn't find me, although the GPS had shown that he had reached my position. Right through the night he had circled my given position without seeing me; and by morning there was a big enough sea running to hide me in the troughs. That's why the Australians had returned to find me and drop smoke floats. Pete told me afterwards that without these, he doubted whether he would ever have found me.

The nightmare was over: Pete had come! I saw *Aqua Quorum* slicing through the crests towards me. The mast seemed OK, and he was under storm jib alone. No problems with the boat, then. The only difficulty remaining was for me to get aboard. I removed my gloves, and started gathering my treasures together. Pete was making a careful approach; real professional work. As he brought me under his lee, I saw that he'd rigged knotted grab ropes at each stanchion. That, in itself, in those conditions couldn't have been easy.

There remained only the last stage to perform: that wasn't going to be easy either, in my weakened state and with a big sea running. *Aqua Quorum* nudged against the raft. Pete was there on deck, and overhead my Australian guardian angel still circled. We didn't say a word as he made the raft fast alongside. I passed the beacons and my food up to him.

'Come on, now.'

'Wait,' I replied in English, and reached for the bottle of champagne.

You should have seen his face – he took the bottle with a disbelieving look in his eyes. It was then that I realised that he was pretty exhausted too; not surprising considering the efforts he must have made to work up to where I was, and he'd been sailing her manually all night. I unhooked my harness from the raft, and stood up, but he grabbed its line and hooked onto his own guardrails. He was absolutely right to do so – who knows what the result of my falling in, un-attached, at this point might have been?

Waiting until the crest lifted the raft, he seized my lifting becket, and hauled me aboard. I rolled onto the deck, and he half-lifted me and pulled me aft. Neither of us spoke. He helped me below and left me there for a moment or two, while he raised the aircraft. They must have been on station for some time, after all, and were operating a good 2500 kilometres from their base.

'I've got Raphael aboard. He's OK but chilled. Everything's OK, you can go home now – and thanks.'

Later on, he was to fax to the race organisers:

'Hi, Philippe. Best possible Christmas present. Raphael aboard. Very cold but happy. Not injured. Have his beacons aboard. Cheers. Pete.'

Having reassured the Australians that all was well, though, he returned to me. We quite simply fell into one another's arms in sheer relief. Then there was work to do. I had to get out of my salt-encrusted survival suit, which was burning my skin where the edges of the hood met my face. With Pete's help, I removed this and the rest of my clothing, and asked if he had any baby wipes. This wasn't a silly question, as they are widely used in high latitude sailing where water temperatures are very low. Pete helped me to wash; I didn't have the energy to do it properly myself. Then I went below from the doghouse. After *Algimouss*, it was small; *Aqua Quorum*, at 50 ft LOA, was in fact the smallest boat taking part in the race.

Pete examined my feet, which still had no sensation. He seemed concerned about them, and so was I. He got me a dry polar suit, and helped me into his warmest sleeping bag, even finding me a hot water bottle which he swore had been his grandmother's!

'And now for a cup of tea...'

It was as though I had landed in England! He put a cyclist's water bottle of hot tea into my hands, which were still frozen, nails blackened by frost. I think it was only then that I fully realised that I was saved.

Meanwhile, Pete was up on deck recovering his lifelines and casting off the liferaft. He had already asked the Australians what he should do about it, and they had replied, 'Leave it.'

Looking about me, it came to me just how lucky I was to be here – and how lucky it was that a boat had been anywhere near here at all. It was chaos below, though, as Pete's stores had been more tightly packed than mine, being a smaller boat with no lazarette, and he had suffered nearly twenty knockdowns while racing to my rescue! Pete's wife had made up similar ready meals to mine, but not all the packaging had stood up to the violent shocks. On top of all that a number of leaks had started. It had been a huge struggle to get here, and *Aqua Quorum* showed clear signs of what she had been through.

Having sorted things out on deck and set his storm jib to draw, Pete set a course for Australia. He was exhausted by the time he came below, and crashed out on the berth opposite mine. We would not move about greatly for the next forty-eight hours. The sea was getting up as a new depression blew in, but Pete simply wasn't up to returning on deck, despite the fact that the repeated knockdowns had caused a fair amount of damage, including broken battens and seized winches. For two days, we would eat and drink, rest and, of course, talk.

I think we both needed to talk of our experiences, to exorcise some of the fear. I started to explain what had happened, and he interrupted, 'You're a lucky man.' He could very well understand what I had been through. He had been through hellish conditions himself. And yet, the day before, he had faxed to the organisers:

'Hi, Philippe. Sorry to have had nothing to tell you. Survival situation here all night. Knocked down every half-hour or so by huge breaking seas. Wind has eased, but I have sustained damage. Going as fast as I can, and hope to be able to do better shortly. Any news of Raphael? What was his last position? Send me a weather bulletin for the next 12 hours. Cheers. Pete. PS – Happy Christmas.'

He had also advised Jeantot, it turned out later, that he was considering sending a distress message himself. This was what I had feared might happen when I realised that he would have to work to windward. What he did was heroic, and that's no exaggeration. But now I had to tell him what had happened.

The Southern Ocean has a way of making its presence felt, however. Another storm came our way and threw us about in its turn. Under minimal canvas, *Aqua Quorum* was less steady than she would otherwise have been, and we were rattled about. Her state of the art carbon fibre hull was far less easy at sea than *Algimouss*, with her relatively shock-absorbent Kevlar/foam construction. The crashes and noises were more violent, more frightening.

Pete described to me the tremendous impacts *Aqua Quorum* had withstood when working to windward to my rescue, and I could well believe it. The first night aboard I suffered nightmares, and Pete came to reassure me that it was all right. I think at that stage he was afraid too; the shocks and lurches recalled his own repeated knockdowns. I began to talk of what had happened, not too coherently, but he just let me go on, listening right through. I would go over the same events again, I know, and patiently he would listen again.

For the moment, we talked or slept, and let the boat fend for herself. I was exhausted, and Pete was tired out and stressed. The cabin was still a wreck. We were inundated with fax messages, but Pete replied for the moment only to the medical enquiries from Jean-Yves Chauve, the race medical officer.

An ex-Marine, Pete's own paramedical knowledge was good. From 27 December he would send back regular situation reports on my medical state. My feet were the main cause for concern; I was relieved when, although still without feeling, I began to be able to move my toes again. My hands had seized, and I couldn't really close them. Pete worked superbly on my hands, feet and eyelids, following Jean-Yves' directions. I felt great confidence in the care I was receiving. Not only was Pete my doctor, he was my nurse as well: my frozen and disrupted system made my first trips to the heads a nightmare, apart from which my weakened legs obliged Pete to assist me. It was the kind of total care I shall never forget.

There remained an initial language barrier, at least to a small extent. While Virginie's English is good, mine at that stage was limited. I had been able to understand the met information and other regular messages in English, but the written language is always easier. And now I found myself with a skipper who spoke no French at all! Extraordinarily, though, the words seemed to come, and within a few days I was able not only to understand but to reply. I couldn't walk, could hardly move, but was communicating in a foreign language which I'd never found easy. I can only think our fantastic friendship kindled out of shared horrors must have been the catalyst.

• CHAPTER 15 •

High latitude proposal

Pete was patient with me for the first two days. Then, like a good medic, he got down to work. First I had to get up, and take a few steps with his help. Then came exercises. I had to stretch my muscles, to move tired and inflamed joints, and was not allowed back into my bunk until he judged I could stand no more. Day by day the exercises got harder, but day by day I made progress. He was pleased, and said as much to the doctor. I don't think he was as pleased as I was.

While I was crashed out after an exercise session, Pete would go up on deck to do necessary repairs. There were plenty of them to occupy him. Now we were heading north towards the Australian coast, where he planned to put in at Hobart, Tasmania. It was further than Fremantle, which was the nearest port, but Pete knew Hobart already from the Sydney–Hobart race. He had friends there, and as he was without detailed landfall charts, it was better to go somewhere a little familiar. One additional problem for him would be that the race regulations forbade him to go ashore or to accept assistance, and he intended to comply with this to the letter – after all, one outsider aboard was enough!

Once my hands were working again, I sent the first fax since my rescue to Virginie:

'Dearest love – Marvellous to be able to write to you again. Difficult for me to be able to tell you about the last few days, as I want to wipe them from my memory, and only have good things to look forward to. Pete has decided to put me ashore at Hobart, Tasmania. He has friends there. What I'd like – I don't know if it can be done – is that you should be waiting for me there. It would be fantastic. All my clothes and papers are gone. I don't want to come home like a tramp. If you can meet me we could spend a few quiet days together, before I have to face the journalists and sponsors. Love you more than ever. Give Little'un a big kiss for me.'

As soon as news of my rescue had got through, Virginie had sent a fax thanking Pete. On 29 December he replied:

'Hi, Virginie – A great pleasure to have saved Raphael, and to be meeting you in a few days. We'll drink a glass or six together on my return from the race. Raphael getting better every day, though still stiff and exhausted. He's asleep at present, but he hasn't forgotten that it's your birthday today, and wants to write to you when he wakes. I don't know if he's told you, but I'm taking him to Hobart and I think if you were there it would start the healing process for both of you after a bad experience. Can you be there, if it's possible, for our arrival? Raphael is still unwell and I think that a few days with you in Tasmania will ease the strain of his having to face the publicity circus.'

Good old Pete! He had thought of everything. I'd said to him, 'The 29th is Virginie's birthday; can you make sure I don't forget it, because I don't feel sure about what day it is? Not like her – she has the memory of an elephant. You know, years after the event she'll remember a particular evening, what I did and everything else. So if I once forget her birthday...' And Pete had duly entered it in his log.

Wedged before the keyboard, I found my mind wandering back to the fax I had sent on the 24th, how I had regretted having forgotten about the Christmas presents, and I had promised her a surprise for my return. Well, my return had been brought forward, and I decided the surprise must be brought forward too.

'My love – Hope you're having a fabulous birthday. A very big kiss. I hope I'm coming over coherently because I've something very special to ask you. I was trying to work round to it in my Christmas fax from *Algimouss*, so I think you can guess what it is. Can we have Little'un christened, and get married on my return? Do tell her I'm coming home, and give her lots of big kisses for me... See you soon, darling.'

Shortly afterwards, Virginie replied: 'Yes, yes! Marvellous. And I want Pete to be best man.'

I told Pete that I had asked Virginie to marry me, that she had said 'Yes,' and wanted him to be our best man. We threw our arms around one another. Imagine – proposing by satellite from beyond the 50th parallel, and with my rescuer as best man. What a story! I sent a very short fax to Virginie: 'Pete will be best man.'

It was time to open the champagne.

Over the next few days there followed a torrent of communications. Family, friends, sponsors, journalists... Everyone thanked Pete, my parents saying that they now thought of him as part of the family. One touching fax came from my elder brother, who now lived in Paris, so we didn't see each other anywhere near as often as we would have liked: 'It looks as though we have another brother now in Pete.'

There were other touching messages too; I tried to translate them to Pete in my limited English. He listened attentively, and I'm sure he understood very well. The fax was in operation 24 hours a day, and I swear the computer was running hot. I still found it an effort to get myself to the keyboard to reply, not least because, in this smaller boat, there was no operator's chair; I had to type standing. Pete sorted out a solution involving a full sailbag lashed in place, on which I reclined like a Roman emperor. I found sitting up for any length of time difficult, so he rigged a cushion I could lash to my chest and which rested against the work-top to prop me in position. No matter how it looked, it worked.

What it couldn't solve, of course, were the other problems: the difficulty of focusing my salt-burned eyes, or the fact that as the circulation returned to my fingers, they inevitably swelled until I was effectively unable to type, and remained so for two days. Then, of course, the computer began to suffer from the damp atmosphere – not altogether surprising in the circumstances! In the end, I tapped out painfully, 'Taking a break!' and hoped it would get through.

Eventually, the long-suffering communications equipment did in fact give up. It wasn't altogether a misfortune, as the drain on our batteries and demands on the generator for recharging were getting beyond a joke. In any case, it was becoming tiring to be trapped by the media, unable to get away. Pete showed greater strength of character in this than me; if he felt it necessary, he would ignore a fax which had arrived and didn't need an immediate reply, leaving it for later when he felt like responding. I got some measure in this of the man's inner strength; a Best Man in more ways than one.

As we talked, I discovered that Pete had experienced diffi-culties similar to my own. He had sold his house to pay for his boat, and had rented another, but with the freezing conditions that had gripped England and much of the rest of Europe for more than six weeks, Pete's wife didn't know how they were going to pay for their heating. For this reason, it seemed that she and their children would not be able to come to Les Sables d'Olonne for Pete's return. Shortly afterwards one of Pete's sponsors came up with the expenses for this, and Pete was deliriously happy, forgetting for the moment the £75,000 deficit he was running for the boat and campaign.

I should say that Pete is very much a family man. His navigation space was plastered with drawings and poems from his three children, aged from four to twelve years. It was something I greatly looked forward to, and something else we had in common. We also discovered a shared pleasure in music, and this in strange circumstances: his cassette player was out of action, but he had a walkman set in working order. However, the same storm which had doused the cassette player had wrecked his tapes. As I became mobile again, I began to put his stores in order, and in doing so found a number of tapes which had been hidden away for him to discover as surprise presents. I was very happy also to find him a letter with Christmas greetings from his children, which brought tears of joy to his eyes.

By now we were approaching New Year's Day, and neither of us had eaten a Christmas dinner. Sorting out the supplies, I turned up Pete's Christmas pudding, which he had forgotten. We had also set aside my champagne bottle from the liferaft, but I didn't know whether the small amount left would be drinkable. However, I'm an optimist. We had Christmas pudding, champagne and music. No turkey: but there were the half-dozen preserved meals I'd saved from the liferaft. I suggested that Pete try one, and he was delighted. 'You mean you can bring food like this to sea?' I explained that Virginie had prepared a supply of them so that I could eat well on my voyage. 'Well, next time,' he replied, 'I'm taking French supplies with me!' I was gratified that it pleased him so much. He had a supply of half-bottles of wine, so we were able to enjoy a new year celebration despite the gale and the buffeting.

One evening, when the last of my ready meals had been eaten, Pete announced a surpise. That was fine, but rather puzzling; I wondered what sort of a surprise it could be. As I watched, he poured some oil into a saucepan and added a handful of kernels of some kind. Whatever was he making for me?

'Got it, Pete! Popcorn?'

'That's right!'

He was really pleased. As a little lad, I had made popcorn with my sister. Now I remembered it, and this is what he was doing. It was a comforting thought.

'No sugar or salt?' I asked. There was in fact neither in any case, as they had both been spoilt by salt water. While I waited, doubtfully considering the lack of these essentials, Pete told me a story, possibly detecting my mistrustful look. Since setting out, he had made popcorn quite often on the little American cooker he used, which I don't doubt stood up to salt water well enough, but was to my way of thinking downright dangerous. It was really nothing more than an Army mess tin on a camping gas stove! Aboard *Algimouss*, I'd had a proper galley, fully equipped.

Well, to cut a long story short, it seemed that one day he had been making popcorn, but had gone up on deck to carry out some adjustments, and had returned below to find popcorn all over the place. The corns had exploded and plastered themselves all over everything – the navaids display, the radar screen, the lot! We both roared with laughter at the thought of it. Now we were two-handed, though, there was no chance of it happening a second time.

'OK, it's good popcorn,' I told him. I imagined that it was a snack before our meal, the kind of thing which in France we nibble with aperitifs. As soon as it was ready, he offered me a bowlful.

'Hell, Pete, you know I won't be able to eat that much...' but to please him, I took a handful. With neither salt nor sugar it was more than enough. Meanwhile, he had eaten all the popcorn in his bowl. I didn't want any more, and offered him the remainder of mine. He was delighted, and wolfed it down. Then I realised. This wasn't a snack, it was our evening meal. Popcorn with no salt – the mad Brit!

I had a suggestion to make.

'Look, Pete, I've an idea. I'm French, and maybe a bit Italian, and I can cook. You look to the boat and I'll look to our food.'

He was pleased enough. Until then, food had been a simple matter of refuelling, but then he had tried Virginie's meals, which seemed a good first step. As I became mobile and a little more fit, I made a start. There were some onions, not in a very good state, but a great deal can be done with onions to improve basic food, especially pasta. I began to sort through the supplies a little further. Some had been ruined, but there were sauces, Italian style even though they were 'Made in England'. Very well, I could do something with them too.

When I saw what Pete had been eating all along, I was shocked. His wife had made him up a daily ration of treats – crisps, nutty bars, chocolate and so on, and he had been living mainly on these. He explained to me that he was used to this, along with pub snacks. I decided I could show him that there were better things in life, and got to work with the pasta and sauces. When he had time, I taught him some culinary tricks as well. As he had obtained the race organisers' consent to take on additional stores at Hobart, I suggested that Virginie assist, and Pete jumped at the idea. I think his culinary conversion was a considerable contribution to international understanding in the history of deep-sea sailing.

• CHAPTER 16 •

'We two...'

So, it was New Year's Eve, and time for a celebration. The conditions had eased, as if the weather too was in celebratory mood. The champagne was cooling in the bilge, there was Christmas pudding, and Pasta Dinelli on the stove.

Among Pete's presents, we had found some funny party hats; for Pete a bobble hat with silly motifs sewn on, and for me a pair of earphones holding together a Christmas cracker and the word BANG! Midnight approached; as soon as it was New Year, I would send greetings to Virginie. Once again I had left her all the problems of moving house. This was our fourth move, and each time I had been at sea. Perhaps in one respect she prefers it this way, as I have a terrible tendency to throw things out. Virginie is the opposite: she hangs onto everything, her things and mine; it had become something of a joke between us. I could probably live from a rucksack in the back of my van for years; she is a home-maker. This time, though, there had been an additional problem.

She had moved, with the assistance of her coven of girl-friends, a week earlier, and had sent me a fax aboard *Algimouss* with our new phone number: this just when the media and sponsors etc were getting to know our old one. She had tried to take the old number with her, but France

Telecom weren't capable of doing anything so simple. I had noted the new number, of course, but this was at the bottom of the sea, and I'm not good at remembering such things. When Pete had rescued me, typically, the first thing he had said was, 'I'll contact your wife right now to let her know you're safe.' Oh, Christ! I explained that she had just moved and I couldn't remember the new number. His reply was my first taste of British humour. 'Here – you are the bloody skipper, aren't you – not a stowaway?'

We were to get to know one another extremely fast because of the nature of the circumstances of our meeting. I know it's said that seafarers do so easily in any case, but we found that we share a philosophy of life and an understanding of the sea. He is older than I am, and with wider experience of the world and of life, but I suppose I had been through a great deal of experience too. I think the first two days, when we were both exhuasted and could in fact do little but talk, had acted as a powerful catalyst. We are both fanatics when it comes to boats, and Pete had built his own: he was extremely proud to show me her constructional details, his own personal trademarks. I can really believe that he loves that boat.

Then too, those who share the closed, concentrated world of a small boat on a great ocean learn to share a great deal of one another. Take the morning when I heard him bellowing like a madman up on deck. Sticking my head out of the companionway hatch, I saw him at the wheel, steering manually, and cracking an imaginary whip over an imaginary chariot team! *Aqua Quorum* was planing like a beauty, and there he was at the reins of his chariot. The crazy Brit. Magnificent.

We were to spend many hours discussing boats and seafaring, particularly the technical side. We made sketches of the way our ideas were going, ideas we should like to incorporate in our future boats. We worked on the safety factor, too; we had both had hair's breadth escapes, and I think that after this experience, safety became something of an obsession. I even found myself dreaming of such things, and would commit them to paper on wakening. We worked together on these projects; aerofoil masts, lifting keels, and many other things. We found we both felt there should be better Franco-British co-operation, not only at sea but in the maritime world as a whole. We have, after all, a great deal to offer each other.

'You know,' I found myself saying to Pete, 'The real problem is the French mentality.' This interested him. I went on to explain that while French skippers outnumber other nations in ocean racing, I felt that they were too individualistic, too secretive, when there was a great deal they had discovered which would be of great use and importance to others. Yves Parlier, for example, a leading specialist in the computerisation of autopilots; Christophe Auguin, Isabelle Autissier, specialists in their own fields, but keeping their inventions as their own personal secrets. And that is the French way; in the big league, a great deal of espionage goes on as a result of it.

Now this may be all very well in racing, but in terms of safety at sea, it is lunacy. Can you imagine the inventor of the ABS braking system keeping it as a secret to be used only on his own car? Further down the racing hierarchy you do not find this mentality, but these people are under less pressure from their sponsors and the media. It's comparable in some ways with motor racing: but the sea is not a race circuit, and has a way of punishing this kind of lone wolf mentality. When we challenge the sea, we should do so united.

We found, too, that we felt the French and British racing worlds were too mutually exclusive, and that there should be more of an exchange, not only of competitors but of ideas too. For our own part, we promised to tour each other round our respective countries; I should be glad of this, as I'm a great admirer of British rigging and deck hardware, and of British electronics.

Pete seemed less concerned than he had been about the Vendée Globe challenge. He knew he had lost his position in the race. I knew it was my fault, and tended to blame myself, but Pete didn't reproach me with it. As far as he was concerned, it was now simply a question of taking me to Hobart, after which he would rejoin the race: as simple as that. And that is the true measure of Pete: he could simply have taken me aboard as so much extra ballast and rejoined the race, signalling for me to be winched up by a chopper when next convenient.

It wasn't that he had lost interest in the race itself, of course; far from it. We continued to follow the daily race bulletins, although it felt odd, and sad, to see that I had disappeared from the news. Understandable, but there you are. The news now was of concern for the fate of Gerry Roufs. We would learn more of this on our arrival in Tasmania.

We talked, then, of many things, and only in one story that I told did we not really see eye to eye; the tale of the albatross attacking the raft and the beacons. It seemed to threaten to destroy for him the image, common in seafaring folklore, of the great birds as a good omen. 'Does he not believe that it happened?' I asked myself; and then, shortly afterwards, he too had an odd experience with an albatross. I was below in my bunk when I heard an excited shout of, 'Raphael, Raphael!'

What was it? I feared the worst, perhaps naturally after my experience. Had he injured himself? Pete wouldn't shout excitedly for nothing, I was aware of that, and of how calm he could be during difficult manoeuvres. I distinctly remembered the time when, after a difficult gybe, he came below to reassure me that all was well. And now he was shouting to me urgently. I crawled up the companionway – we were pitching badly – to find him laboriously hauling up his overtrousers, face contorted with mirth. What had gone on? It transpired that Pete dislikes marine heads, and will only use them when conditions are too foul to go on deck, preferring the rail. He had just completed his morning performance when he was startled by an albatross diving right alongside, thinking this was a new sort of fish! So now, even if he didn't think albatross were vicious, at least he knew they were complete idiots.

I think this view of the albatross would have shocked Philippe Jeantot, and probably Bernard Moitessier as well. For them, the albatross was the mysterious, almost enchanted bird which would follow a ship right round the Antarctic Circle. I was to learn, though, that this romantic view was far from universal. In Tasmania I heard that the old sailing ship seamen hated them for the way they would attack a man in the water, going first for the eyes; I was told that the old shellbacks would be more likely to shoot them than to sentimentalise over them, and I could now understand this perfectly well.

As the days passed, I could feel a change in myself: perhaps this wasn't unexpected after the experiences I had been through, but I think it was my long conversations with Pete which really brought my thoughts together in concrete form, as we talked of the sea, of religion, of food, of relationships. He talked modestly of the things he had seen and learned, of his time in the Far East with the Royal Marines, and of the interest in Eastern religion which it had awakened in him.

I have the greatest respect for Pete; I feel that I have learned a great deal from him, and that his experience has been much wider than mine. Not that he has been simply a mentor; he has changed my life. I have learned, too, from his rich cultural background, which made me feel that mine, up to that point, had been poor. He is like many British people, whose culture is rich, and not only the culture of the sea. I had read far less on this subject than Pete, never really liking old sailors' reminiscences because I had felt that my seagoing adventures were my own, and I did not want a point of comparison; perhaps this is no more than an excuse for always having been disinclined to read anything unnecessary from a professional point of view.

Now I, too, wanted to share in the inherited culture of the sea. I've always liked old ports and historic ships, with the tales they have to tell, and this wouldn't take over at all from my state-of-the-art techniques; it would coexist with them. I spoke of this to Pete, that I would continue in my search for speed and reliability, and I would embark on another Vendée Globe – but this time there would be one difference. I would read more, much more, and I would have a fund of maritime culture to sail with me.

Just consider: in these modern boats, with computer aided navigation, the singlehanded operation of a yacht is no longer a 24 hour per day business, and the race can last three months. There is time to spare, and during this time it may be possible to escape from the strain of the race. Now if this free time were enriched by reading, or by thinking of what one has read, it could be a great contribution to the lone skipper's wellbeing.

It seemed to me, too, that a storehouse of culture is a great possession for an ageing sailor; when I finally swallow the anchor, I will want a treasury of tales to combine with my own. It occurred to me, for example, that a navigator who follows, say, the Vikings' sea lanes shares a certain amount with them. Those ancient mariners set out without charts, let alone GPS, with no weather service to call on and no means of contact with home; but the sea itself is the same for the sailor of 1997 as it was for them. A Dark Ages sea ran as high, and broke as heavily, as a sea today. We survive most of the time; how many of them did not? And back then it took them more than a month to cover the same distance that can be sailed in a few days by today's best ocean racers. A voyage of exploration might take them months or years. When I felt low I could talk with Virginie; we could shed tears together. What of the separation those long-ago sailors had to endure?

We don't even have to go back as far as the Viking age for a similar comparison; consider what sailing ship seamen went through, in some cases less than a lifetime ago. Yes, it makes me feel that my experiences were very small beer. I'm not trying to detract from today's advances in seafaring, simply to set them in context. But, you know, it was a context I might never have so much as considered without Pete's influence.

• CHAPTER 17 •

Can you smell the gum trees?

Pete knew very well that our arrival in Hobart would be difficult for me on account of the inevitable media harassment. He advised me to get in as much sleep as I could during the last 48 hours of our approach to the Tasmanian coast. For my part, I was feeling much better, not least for knowing that Virginie would be there. There was one problem, however, in that Pete had no chart aboard of the approaches to Hobart. I'd taken a full set of landfall charts with me, just in case of such an emergency, but Pete hadn't reckoned on making landfall anywhere except at the end of the race. This was the very reason, of course, why he had chosen Hobart as our landfall, a port he remembered, even though it involved sailing 1500 miles further than the nearest port of Fremantle. 'Raphael,' he had explained, 'It's going to take a good six days more, but it will be safer if we go to Hobart. I'm sorry for Virginie, but it makes more sense this way.'

I knew he was right, of course. Even as it was, our approach to Hobart called for the utmost caution, equipped as we were only with passage charts. The last stages were very much in the tradition of Lead, Lookout and Log. Pete raised Hobart control, and giving his position, asked for a course to clear the reefs. That final night neither of us slept;

the approaches are guarded by rocks which lie only just awash. Meanwhile, Pete also raised the Marine Rescue ComCen at Canberra, and managed to speak to Sam, the Australian who had supervised my rescue and was to become yet another friend.

In the early hours of the morning, the wind and sea got up again; 35 knots and a 4 to 5 metre sea, in the trough of which we snatched occasional menacing glimpses of reefs lying in wait. So much for the sunny beaches of Australia! Pete typically cracked a joke: 'Well, Raphael, at least you've done this before, so stick your survival suit on.'

'Come on, now, Pete,' I replied, 'once is quite enough!' And so we made our approach. Later we were told that we must have passed no more than a hair's breadth from a number of notorious reefs.

Finally, land hove in sight.

'Can you smell the eucalyptus?' Pete asked. I was puzzled, assuming that he was speaking of eucalyptus cough sweets. He explained. 'It's said that when you approach the coast of Australia, you will always smell the eucalyptus trees.' Then he warmed to his subject: 'And just think, you'll be able to eat your first Australian steak and drink Aussie beer!' He had been dreaming of this for days; English (or Australian) breakfast, T-bone steaks and burgers. There was a far-away look in his eyes. 'Raphael, just think about what you'll be able to eat and drink here!'

Poor Pete, the race rules insisted that he must not set foot ashore! Then, of course, down there it was summer. Here we were, 44 degrees south, 40 degrees Celsius and I could see distant palm trees. Yet just 6 degrees of latitude south of here there had been icebergs and the water temperature just nudging zero... all this difference in a mere 600 kilometres. In terms of actual distance sailed from where I had been rescued, it had been 3000 kilometres and 12 extraordinary days.

We were determined to make the best of that last day before the media could get to us, but it was not to be. The sky was now teeming with aircraft and choppers, and it felt at times as though we were under attack as one or two narrowly missed our mast. One, from Australian television, did its best to put a rotor tip through our mainsail, and this while I gave the journalist inside my first radio interview! I suppose I owed it to Australian TV, the Australians having masterminded my rescue. I must say, I hadn't expected such a near miss, though.

'Raphael – look at all these boats!' With the games the aircraft had been playing, we had hardly noticed the power-boats which were closing us. We were still quite some distance out to sea, but apart from the media and the Australian officials, everyone with a boat seemed to have put out to meet us, and some of them did not appear to be the world's best seamen!

Pete reduced sail for easier manoeuvring and hung out every fender he had. We felt just like a stagecoach surrounded by galloping Indians. We had planned to try to keep the media at arms' length initially, but it was down-right impossible in these circumstances, with boatloads of photographers whizzing round us, and the fax and VHF gibbering a constant stream of English and French. We felt we hardly knew where we were.

Amid the stream of messages, we picked up Sam from Canberra with news of Bullimore and Dubois, then the final approach instructions from Hobart control. That was enough, and Pete had had enough. He switched off both sets and relative silence fell. All our concentration was focused on keeping the boat safe from these fools.

In the end, I asked Pete if I could remain aboard for another 24 hours. 'OK, Raphael, quite understood.' And with that I went below to make tea and slice up a fruit cake which I had found in the stores, and which turned out to be a present from Pete's grandmother. Under easy sail we jogged on, taking our five o'clock tea, smiling royally to the cameras and extended microphones, otherwise ignoring them. Pete was quite cool, too, towards the harbourmaster's crew, one of whom came aboard with a towline. 'Not yet. We've all the time in the world,' said Pete. They then asked for me to come aboard the launch. Pete replied firmly that I would come ashore when we reached port. And so it was that we had another two hours to talk of the future and say our farewells.

'What do you plan to do right now?' he asked. 'Will you go straight back to France? I think you ought to give yourself a breathing space. You've nothing more to prove to yourself.' I suspect Pete knows me better than I know myself.

Finally, it was time to go; I felt as if I were jumping ship. The harbourmaster's launch had returned, and I didn't doubt there were all sorts of forms to be filled in. We didn't make a performance of saying goodbye, just embraced silently, as we had when Pete had first hauled me aboard from the life-raft. I didn't look back.

And now there was a new storm to be faced; a storm of publicity – and this storm didn't stop for a full twenty-four hours. Much later, or so it seemed, I returned exhausted to the harbour. Borrowing a dinghy, I went in search of Pete, as I suspected he would have been concerned for me at the effect of the sort of media interrogation he knew I would have faced.

Virginie had not been on any of the welcoming fleet. We had agreed that it would be better this way, and might give us a chance to escape the worst of the media attention, which she found distressing. Suffice to say that we had been offered a small cottage, tucked away in a quiet corner not too far from Hobart, and there we spent the next few days, quite simply recovering. We also found that there were discoveries to be made in this new world which was quite different from our native France; Pete had asked us to go to an Australian pub and drink to his own safe return, and so, as soon as the opportunity arose, that is just what we did.

We found a cheerful-looking pub, where an equally cheerful waitress brought us T-bone steaks with chips, and of course Pete's Aussie beer. We drank to him as we had promised.

Australia had more surprises in store. Everything seemed to be huge, not least the fruit and vegetables, to say nothing of the meals! The lady who hired us her cottage told us of spiders as big as her hand, but apparently harmless. What a place it was!

Shortly afterwards, I had to go up to Canberra to meet the rescue co-ordinators; it was they who had directed the aircraft to me and orchestrated operations afterwards. And over the twelve days that had followed my rescue we had been in constant contact with Sam. I had never met him, and it was a moving experience for me to greet him at last. He and the rest of the team were fully occupied just then with Tony Bullimore and Thierry Dubois; but I was the first of the Vendée Globe casualties they had seen in the flesh. It must be a strange life they lead. They could perhaps be described as distant seafarers, directing operations which they never saw. They said they had never had such a fraught time, though, as during these Vendée Globe rescues. And here I was, the first of their charges to come ashore. They gave me a hero's welcome, Sam especially. When Virginie arrived they fell into each other's arms, and both wept.

It was extraordinary, here in a Starship Enterprise environment alive with computers and flashing screens, to see the aerial film footage of my rescue down there in the Southern Ocean. I asked the radio operators if I could possibly send a message to Pete, who was already 600 miles out to sea once again. I was able to say only a brief 'Hello Pete!' which would have to suffice until we all met once more.

I was pleased, very pleased, to be shown his position, because it sent me a clear message. At three days out, he had made a good 200 miles a day, very good going in the circumstances. So his race was by no means over. Later, in fact, he was to break all records for 50-footers by putting in an extraordinary 330 miles in a day's run. I had been worried that the time taken to return me to port might have led him to think that the race was over for him as well as me. I don't think I should ever have been concerned on that score. Pete was away again, and with the will to succeed.

• CHAPTER 18 •

Providence and Argos...

The list of those whom I have to thank for having survived is a long one; Pete, Sam, the RAAF aircrew, and many, many others. One I have not yet mentioned though, and whom we should not forget, is called simply Argos. His name derives from the Greek god who could see in all directions. Argos is the name given to the distress beacons to which I owe my life.

The control centre for French beacons is in Toulouse, and it was from there that a technician came up to Les Sables before I set out, to set up and test my beacons. When he asked if I was sure I knew how they worked, I replied with a grin that I had sailed three Figaros and one Transatlantic with beacons aboard, and while, thank goodness, I had not had to use one, I knew how to set them off. I then asked him if he knew Philippe, an old pal who worked for Argos, and who still had a summer bungalow at Arcachon. He was a great follower of ocean racing, and we had met up several times during the Figaro or at St-Barthelémy; it was always an occasion for celebration, too.

'Philippe? He's down in Australia at the moment.'

'Bugger!' I replied. 'That means I'll miss him.' But, of course, it didn't work out that way, thanks to the mother of all waves.

After our stay at Hobart, Virginie and I flew to Melbourne, where we were to stop a while before continuing to Canberra. While in Melbourne we were contacted by the French consul, who was organising a dinner in our honour for the following evening. She told us that the French tennis team was staying in the hotel at which she had arranged the meal, and it would be nice if we were to be able to meet them. It appeared that they had followed my story in the newspapers, and had been very concerned for me. At present, they were in training for the Australian Open Championships. I was very happy to be able to meet them, and enjoy a long chat with Guy Forget.

The following day, the consul asked whether I would like to meet a representative of Argos over dinner that evening. I told her the story of the part the beacons had played in my rescue, and added that in the circumstances I would be only too pleased. The Argos representative turned out to be a really charming girl, who found it genuinely moving that their beacons had saved me. Inevitably, I asked her about Philippe. Did she know him, as I had heard that he was currently in Australia? She grinned hugely. 'Oh, yes,' she replied. 'In fact we're getting married in a few months; but at the moment he's back in France.' So we had missed each other once again!

It turned out that she and Philippe were planning to remain in Australia, as Argos were in the process of setting up a second monitoring centre in Perth, at the other end of the country from their existing station in Melbourne. It had been operational for just one month. Our new friend then delivered her punch line: 'Did you know that it was thanks to the new station you were rescued?' She went on to explain that its existence had saved four hours in the process of plotting my position. When you consider that the Australians had succeeded in finding me just before nightfall, and that I would most certainly not have survived the night without their help, I literally owed these people my life. So here was yet another member of the team who had helped to save me. You can imagine the gratitude I expressed; and here, almost at the end of my story, I thank them all again.

Les Sables d'Olonne, Sunday 23 March, 1997

Standing at the helm of a launch, I scanned the horizon for a first sight of what will be Pete Goss's masthead. I had wanted to be the first to see him, the first to welcome him. I owed him that. I had thought of little else for weeks now.

It was two and a half months since he had put me ashore in Hobart and shortly afterwards put to sea again. During all that time he had written regularly by fax to Virginie and me; despite all the stress of the race, despite an injured elbow on which he had had to operate himself, a process taking all of six hours – despite all this, he continued to think of us. What an incredible guy.

• 6 February •
Hi, Raphael. Things are going better. Here's to your future, both of you.

• 16 February •
Cape Horn did its worst. I drank to the Horn for you all the same; I'm sure you will round it one day.

• *23 February* •

With all the problems waiting for me ashore, can I ask for your wedding not to take place until June? Then you could come and stay with us in England. I don't know what you have planned for my return, but I've arranged with all my pals and sponsors that we should meet up in the Galway Bar and sink a few jars together. Very glad to hear you're considering another 60-footer. I've no doubt that you'll find one. We must campaign a double-handed race together. We just have to be a winning team.

• *2 March* •

Just 284 miles from the Equator – soon be back in the Northern Hemisphere. It's great, I feel I'm coming home. Have arranged a celebration with my home club for the end of April, and we all want you and Virginie to be there.

• • •

I think these messages give some measure of the man – a friend and a seaman, with a great sense of organisation and of responsibility. In his last message, a few days before his arrival, he asked me for the name of the boat in which I was coming out to meet him so that he could identify me and raise me on VHF. I thought he would have quite enough to attend to when he made landfall, without having to attend to me. All the same, here I was as the afternoon drew on, lying off Les Sables. I found my mind running through another day, when I had seen that yellow hull coming towards me on that hellish sea. I'd found a sweater of the same colour, so that I could wear it today in solidarity; our team colours, as they now were.

Above all, though, this was Pete's day. I had made up my mind to remain firmly in the background. I had seen the crowds gathered to welcome him, a hundred thousand strong; I also remembered his message to the race organisers that he wanted me to be the first aboard when he finally brought *Aqua Quorum* alongside.

For the moment, though, here I was, still scanning the horizon. I knew the direction from which he would come, better, I think than the skippers of the flotilla of boats lying further inshore. Then – I wasn't sure – but on the horizon, wasn't that *Aqua Quorum*'s spinnaker? Right – FULL AHEAD! Behind me, I saw the others heading seaward too.

And there he was – up on deck, typical ex-Marine, spruced up for the big day. I wouldn't have recognised him as the bearded scruff of the Southern Ocean I'd first seen, but of course, because he had company, he'd shaved and smartened up like an English gentleman. He told me afterwards that he had done so using his last disposable razor but one, and when he'd put back to sea he would keep the last so that he could shave again on his return to please his wife; and he had done just this.

Virginie, by my side, wept with emotion. I waved like a madman; and there – yes – he'd seen me! Magnificent. And now, I would escort him home, up the approach channel, with hundreds of other boats now closing in on all sides. We turned aside in the basin, and motored to a vacant berth. Pete was now alongside: I saw Tracey, Pete's wife, go aboard, and they embraced long and lovingly. Then it was time for champagne and cheers. Pete saw me standing, watching, and signalled to Virginie and me to come aboard. Yes, we were just as we had been. I was lost for words; I remember being able to say only that his boat looked smart, far more so than mine ever would.

Half an hour later it was the turn of Catherine Chabaud; and that signified the end. The game had been played, and the Vendée Globe was over. Pete was caught up in the whirl-wind of greetings and press conferences, but that night we would meet, just as planned, in the Galway Bar, and yes, we sank more than a few jars together. The following day we met for breakfast, a Franco-British breakfast, as Pete asked me to bring fresh croissants – he and Tracey would do the rest.

It was a breakfast which was to last all morning. Pete and Virginie talked interminably over the events of that winter, and my shipwreck.

'You know,' she confided to him, 'I feared that you might find an empty liferaft, or Raphael dead inside.' It appeared that he had been troubled by the same thoughts as he beat up to my last known position. And, typically, what had troubled him most, if that had been the case, was 'Whatever should I say to his wife?'

Not that all we spoke of was so gloomy; there was a future to look forward to. Pete planned three months' complete break before considering what next; certainly before considering whether to do Vendée Globe 2000. For the time being it was enough that he would sail *Aqua Quorum* home to England, and start work on a book.

'Hey, Raphael,' he asked, 'why don't you come along with me? It would be a great sail.' I had to reply that I was uncertain whether I could; and by the following day I had established that it would not be possible. Pete was disappointed. His sailing companion, Mark, had laid in a gourmet's store of provisions after Pete had told him that I would probably be sailing this time as cook. He prevailed on me in the end, however, to join him on a short cruise up the coast, and that is where my story ends: once again aboard *Aqua Quorum*. But this time I could take the helm, and when I did, I found myself looking forward to the future, when Pete and I will find ourselves sailing side by side again, working up to the start line to set off around the world for the millennial Vendée Globe.

• INDEX •